HOW TO BEAT ANYONE AT CHESS

HOW TO BEAT ANYONE AT CHESS

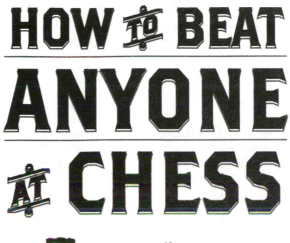

The

BEST CHESS TIPS, MOVES, & TACTICS

to Checkmate

ETHAN MOORE

adamsmedia
Avon, Massachusetts

Published by
Adams Media, a division of F+W Media, Inc.
57 Littlefield Street, Avon, MA 02322. U.S.A.
www.adamsmedia.com

Contains material adapted from *The Everything® Chess Basics Book*, by U.S. Chess Federation and Peter Kurzdorfer, copyright © 2003 by F+W Media, Inc., ISBN 10: 1-58062-586-X, ISBN 13: 978-1-58062-586-9.

ISBN 10: 1-4405-9214-4
ISBN 13: 978-1-4405-9214-0
eISBN 10: 1-4405-9215-2
eISBN 13: 978-1-4405-9215-7

Printed in the United States of America.

10   9   8   7   6   5   4   3   2

Library of Congress Cataloging-in-Publication Data

Moore, Ethan.
How to beat anyone at chess / Ethan Moore.
   pages cm
   ISBN 978-1-4405-9214-0 (pb) -- ISBN 1-4405-9214-4 (pb) -- ISBN 978-1-4405-9215-7 (ebook) -- ISBN 1-4405-9215-2 (ebook)
   1. Chess--Study and teaching. 2. Chess--Problems, exercises, etc. I. Title.
   GV1440.M66 2015
   794.1--dc23
                              2015015393

Cover design by Frank Rivera.
Cover images © Clipart.com.

This book is available at quantity discounts for bulk purchases.
For information, please call 1-800-289-0963.

Contents

Introduction

IT LOOKS SIMPLE.

A board with sixty-four squares of alternating colors. Thirty-two pieces—sixteen pawns, four rooks, four knights, four bishops, and two kings and queens. Two armies facing one another, poised for combat.

It looks simple. And yet . . .

For more than 1,500 years, players have faced one another across the chessboard and fought for victory. As for complexity—well, there are more than 300 billion possible ways to play the first four moves of the game. When you consider the possible combinations of the first ten moves, that number rises to an astounding 169,518,829,100,544,000,000,000,000,000.

Clearly there is a lot more chess to be played.

Chess appeals to people from every part of the globe and in every walk of life. It's been a favorite of kings and queens, of presidents and politicians, as well as of people you meet every day. Today you can find chess players in coffee shops, college dorms, and bars. You can play against someone sitting opposite you or you can battle it out with a player in front of her computer half a world away. You can practice your chess game using an app on your smartphone or laptop. You can play a friendly game with your buddy or challenge yourself and your opponent in a high-stakes timed competition. (There have even been players like the legendary Bobby Fischer, who could play an entire chess game *in his head* without board or pieces in front of him.)

Chess sets themselves can be dazzling works of art, their pieces shaped like anything from jewel-encrusted, medieval kings and queens to Homer and Marge Simpson.

Within this book you'll find out more about the remarkable story of this game. As well, you'll learn the basic moves and some points of chess strategy and tactics. (Hint: Control the center of the board!) You'll discover the biographies of some of the people who have become masters of chess. Finally, you'll get a glimpse into the world of organized chess and find out how you can become part of it.

Chess is warfare without bloodshed. It's one of the best ways ever discovered to sharpen your mind and broaden your experience.

Your move!

Where Did It Come From?

DETERMINING THE ORIGIN OF CHESS can be problematic because the game was not invented out of whole cloth. Rather, it evolved over a long time. Its earliest clear ancestor was a game called chatrang, which emerged in Persia between the fifth and sixth centuries, although some argue that the game's roots lie even further back, perhaps as early as the third century.

Chatrang used a sixty-four-square gameboard with thirty-two pieces. Among these pieces were a king, a minister (later replaced by today's queen), two elephants (in place of today's bishops), two horses, and two *ruhks*, the Persian word for "chariots." There were also eight foot soldiers.

Chatrang spread across Europe, probably carried along the Silk Road, the network of trade routes that stretched from China to the Mediterranean Sea. Along the way, the movement of some of the pieces gradually changed. The object of the game evolved from what today we would call stalemate to the modern checkmate.

The greatest change occurred during the eleventh and twelfth centuries when the minister or vizier was replaced by the queen, which during the next several centuries became the most powerful piece on the board. Some researchers have speculated that this change reflected the strong political role played by many medieval queens.

Once it was firmly established, chess began to be systematically studied. The earliest known chess book was published in 1497: *The Art of Chess* by Luis Ramírez Lucena. Somewhat better known is a work by his contemporary Ruy López de Segura, who first analyzed the popular opening subsequently named for him.

Spanish players may have been among the early superstars of the chess world, but as the game made its way across Europe other masters arose in France, Germany, and Italy. In the nineteenth and twentieth centuries, the center of chess shifted to Russia. Particularly under the Soviets, chess became a national sport, heavily subsidized by the government. Chess teams were fielded for international competition and often seemed unbeatable.

The man who almost singlehandedly broke the Soviet domination of twentieth-century chess was Bobby Fischer, considered by many to be the greatest chess player who ever lived. Fischer, a child prodigy, studied the game intently, memorizing thousands of openings and variations, perfecting tactics that astounded grandmasters. In 1972 he played the top Russian, Boris Spassky, in what was dubbed the "Match of the Century." In a titanic struggle of twenty-one games, Fischer won. Sadly, after reaching the acme of the chess world, Fischer withdrew from society, becoming an often penniless recluse in Southern California and later abroad. He became an obsessive anti-Semite, his passport was revoked, and he stopped participating in international competition. He died in Iceland in 2008.

Since Fischer, there have been many great players, such as the Russians Garry Kasparov and Anatoly Karpov. Top chess performers include people such as Judit Polgár, the strongest female player in recorded history, and Magnus Carlsen, the current world champion, who has an official chess rating of 2876 and had the highest rating ever recorded, at 2882. He is also the third-youngest person ever to become a grandmaster, a feat he accomplished at thirteen (the youngest person to do this was Sergey Karjakin, who became a grandmaster at age twelve).

From its humble origins, chess has spread across the globe. It is truly a universal game.

PART I

THE BASICS

CHAPTER 1

The Board and the Pieces

All right. You're ready to learn chess. In front of you is the chessboard: a square divided up into sixty-four smaller, equally sized squares alternately colored light and dark. Chessboards come in all sorts of sizes and the squares can be almost any color, but most serious players stick to a standard size of about 16–22" per side with 2–2½" checkered squares.

Everyone has sixty-four squares to work with. Half of sixty-four is thirty-two. Therefore, here's your first rule of strategy: If you control thirty-three squares, you will have an advantage. Keep this in mind.

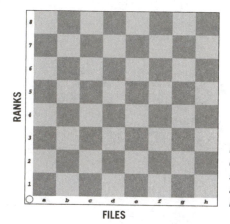

RANKS

FILES

Here is a diagram of a chessboard. Note the checkered squares, and the light square at the right-hand corner at the bottom.

Light on Right

When setting up the chessboard, always make sure a light square is at your lower right corner. Your opponent, who sits opposite you, will also have a light square at his or her lower right corner. (If you prefer, you can think of this as a dark square always being at your left; it works just as well.)

WHAT ARE CHESSBOARDS MADE OF?

The material of a chessboard can be almost anything. Wood, plastic, paper, cardboard, and vinyl are common. So long as there are sixty-four alternating light and dark squares, you have a useable board.

Using All Squares

In chess, both players use all the squares of the board. This is in contrast to the many versions of checkers, where each player only uses half the squares. It also gives special meaning to the appearance of the chessboard in terms of game planning. There are advanced strategies known as *weak-color complexes*, where a player cannot get sufficient control of the squares of one particular color. There is even a chess piece that operates on only one color—the bishop.

Ranks, Files, and Diagonals

The squares of the chessboard do not exist in isolation. They touch or intersect at various points, creating roads or highways across the board. Straight rows of such squares are called *ranks*, *files*, and *diagonals*.

RANKS

As you sit at the chessboard, with a light square at your lower right and a dark square at your lower left, there are eight horizontal rows of eight squares bordering at the sides, stretching from your left to your right. They begin nearest you and wind up nearest your opponent. These rows cover every square on the chessboard, and they are called *ranks*.

Rank Names

Each rank has a name based on how far away it is from you, assuming you are playing the White pieces and your opponent is playing the Black pieces. The rank nearest you is called the *first rank*. The next rank out is called the *second rank*, the next the *third rank*, and so on until you get to the rank nearest your opponent, which is the *eighth rank*. If you are playing the Black pieces, the rank nearest you is the eighth rank and the rank nearest your opponent is the first rank.

What Do Ranks Look Like?

Each rank contains four light squares and four dark squares, which naturally alternate. Each light square borders a dark square, and each dark square borders a light square.

All ranks are not equal. Notice that the first and eighth ranks each border only one rank, while all the other ranks border two ranks. The edge of the board can be a severe restriction in chess, and the first and eighth ranks represent two of those edges.

FILES

As you sit at the chessboard, with a light square at your right and a dark square at your left, there are eight vertical rows of eight bordering squares stretching from you to your opponent. These rows line up from your left to your right and cover every square of the board. These rows are called *files*.

File Names

Each file has a name beginning with a letter and ending with "file." Assuming you are ready to play the White pieces, counting from your left the files are the *a-file*, the *b-file*, the *c-file*, and on to the file furthest to your right (the one starting with the light square), which is the *h-file*.

Assuming you are ready to play the Black pieces, counting from your left the files are the h-file, the g-file, the f-file, and on to the file furthest to your right (the one starting with the light square), which is the a-file.

Diagonals

Ranks and files are not the only highways on the chessboard. There are also the diagonals, which are straight lines made up of individual squares that border at the corners rather than at the sides. They extend at an angle rather than straight across or up and down the board.

There are three main things that distinguish a diagonal from a rank or file:

1. Diagonals border at the corners rather than at the sides.
2. The number of squares in a diagonal varies from two to eight, whereas ranks and files always contain eight squares each.
3. Diagonals consist of squares of one color only, whereas ranks and files always contain an equal mixture of dark and light squares.

Diagonals don't have simple, easy-to-remember names like ranks and files do. But they are sometimes named for the first and last square on the diagonal: The longest dark diagonal can be called the a1–h8 diagonal, while the smallest light-square diagonals can be called the h7–g8 diagonal and the a2–b1 diagonal.

Border

Diagonals border at the corners rather than at the sides of the squares that make them up. This brings up an interesting optical illusion. Look at a chessboard. Consider the a-file and the a1–h8 diagonal. Which is longer?

If you answered the diagonal, you were right in a strictly geometrical sense, but wrong in a chess sense. Each row contains eight squares, and that means they are the same size for the purposes of a chess game. By the same token, it might look like the b1–h7 diagonal is longer than the b-file. But actually it is the file that is longer! The b-file, like all files, contains eight squares, whereas the b1–h7 diagonal consists of only seven squares.

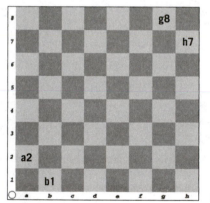

Identifying diagonals.

Size

Thus you can see a very important property of diagonals: They are not even close to being equal. Diagonals are made up of anywhere from two to eight squares. There are four diagonals (two dark and two light) containing two, three, four, five, six, and seven squares, while there are two long diagonals (one dark and one light) that each contain eight squares.

ONE-COLOR DIAGONALS

The most important property of diagonals is that they are all made up of squares of one color. Thus diagonals are limited-access highways compared to ranks and files.

Highways

So far we have learned about four types of roads on the chessboard. If you seem to remember only three, that's because you are not distinguishing between dark-square and light-square diagonals.

Any other highways are mostly ephemeral. Thus you can visualize the route a1–a2–a3–a4–b5–c6–d7–e8. Since all squares border, it is definitely a highway. There are several pieces that could indeed travel this route. But it's actually nothing more than a mixture of the a-file and the a4–e8 diagonal.

RECTANGULAR CORNER

There is just one other type of highway that you need to know about. Because it doesn't involve bordering squares at all, it's questionable whether it can even be called a highway. It also has no name. So we will call it rectangular corner, since that describes the road (or obstacle course): Visualize a six-square rectangle anywhere on the chessboard. Now visualize opposite corners of that rectangle. That's the rectangular corner. This road is bumpy, perhaps, but it's one you will get to know well.

FIVE HIGHWAYS

To review, the five types of chessboard highways are:

- Rank
- File
- Dark-square diagonal
- Light-square diagonal
- Rectangular corner

Square

Not all the squares on a chessboard are created equal, any more than any of the various types of highways are. To begin with, half of them are light and half of them are dark. Of course, there is no essential difference between the dark and light squares.

The real difference between the various squares comes with their neighbors. How many squares does a particular square have bordering it? That's what makes some squares more equal than others.

LOTS OF NEIGHBORS

Those squares that have many bordering squares are in the middle of a metropolis. There are pieces to see, and squares to go to, and activity can be expected to be high. This is simply because there are many different directions that radiate out from such squares.

For example, take a look at e4. There is the fourth rank, the e-file, and the b1–h7 and h1–a8 diagonals. In addition, the rectangular corners available from e4 are f6, g5, g3, f2, d2, c3, c5, and d6. Count up all the squares on major highways directly available from e4 and you will come up with an astounding thirty-five squares, or more than half the chessboard!

WATCH THE CENTER!

The geometrical center of the board (comprised of squares e4, d4, e5, and d5) is where the most traffic will take place. The "greater center" of squares, encompassing c3–c6–f6–f3 and back to c3 and the center squares, usually encounters the next busiest activity. This is because these squares lead directly and quickly to anywhere.

THE EDGE OF THE BOARD

On the other hand, take a look at the edge of the board. Anywhere along the a-file, the h-file, or the first or eighth rank will do. These squares all have some neighbors, but not nearly as many as those in our booming metropolis.

The Pieces and the Pawns

Now that you understand the basic features of the chessboard, we'll move along to the pieces you'll be playing with. Before we do so, though, it's important to understand a basic piece of chess terminology:

1. *Pawns* are the small chess pieces with rounded tops (at least in standard chess sets). At the beginning of the game, white pawns sit on the second rank while black pawns are on the seventh rank.
2. *Pieces* are the larger and generally more powerful chess pieces. There are eight of them: king, queen, two bishops, two knights, and two rooks. White's pieces at the start of a game sit on the first rank while Black's are on the eighth rank.

When chess players talk about "pieces," they're not talking about all chess pieces (including pawns) but *only* these eight that are stronger and generally more important.

All games of chess begin with White making a move. In reply, Black makes a move, and then it's White's turn again. The players continue alternating moves until one of a number of situations occurs that ends the game.

A move in chess is generally defined as a move by White and Black's reply. A single move by White or Black with no reply is usually called a half-move.

BLACK ON TOP

On a computer screen or in a book or magazine, the board is almost always set up so that the White pieces are on the bottom and the Black pieces are at the top. There is no particular reason for this other than tradition. You could just as easily have the Black pieces at the bottom and the White pieces at the top.

The White pieces are set up along the first rank. The rooks begin at the outside corners, with the knights inside, the bishops next, and the king and queen in the middle. The White pawns line up on the second rank. The Black pieces begin on the eighth rank, and the Black pawns begin on the seventh rank. Kings are opposite each other on the e-file and queens are opposite each other on the d-file.

WHERE'S THE KING?

Kings start out on the e-file. Just remember King Edward, and you'll never forget. The queens start out on the d-file. Queen Dolores will do. Also, remember that the queen always starts on her own color: The White queen starts out on d1, a light square, while the Black queen begins on d8, a dark square.

Setting up a chessboard.

The King

Although there are six types of chessmen, the game of chess is really about the king. All other pieces and pawns are there as the king's helpers or weapons. The twin objectives of a chess game are to trap the opposing king and to keep your own king free. This twin objective is probably what makes chess unique. Most other games are measured in accumulations of points or time or territory.

THE STAUNTON DESIGN

Chess pieces have been designed to look like all kinds of things. This is fine for collections and displays. But for practical play, a design is needed that is at once easily recognizable by anyone who plays and readily available. That is the Staunton design, named after its inventor, nineteenth-century Shakespearean scholar and chess master, Englishman Howard Staunton.

POSSIBLE MOVES

The chess king is not particularly strong or fast. He can move in any direction, along a rank, file, or diagonal, one square at a time. This may not sound very promising, but your monarch can have a lot of power late in the game when there are not too many other pieces around. He can have up to eight possible moves in the middle of the board, but only three possible moves from any corner.

Nonetheless the king is extremely valuable: Get him trapped and you lose the game. Therefore, good players often begin by hiding their big guy in an inaccessible corner, while attacking with other pieces and pawns.

CAPTURES

Although the king never leaves the board during a chess game, he can capture other pieces. As long as the enemy piece is within range of the king (that means one square in any direction from where the king stands), he has the option of moving to the square occupied by the enemy piece and removing it from the board.

The Rook

The piece that looks like a tower is often incorrectly referred to as a *castle* by the uninitiated. But by any name, it is a powerful piece to have in your army, and a formidable enemy.

The rook moves along empty ranks or files. Place it on a1 on an empty board and it has fourteen possible moves, anywhere along the a-file or the first rank. Place it on e4 and it can go in four different directions: left along the fourth rank, right along the fourth rank, up (toward your opponent) along the e-file, or down (toward you) along the e-file.

The many possible squares the rook can move to give it a particularly rapid striking capacity. It is indeed a very similar piece to the chariot it was derived from. The rook started out as a chariot or a boat. It became a tower on a siege engine during the Middle Ages.

CAPTURES

The rook can capture any enemy piece (except the king) or pawn in its path. And although it is not possible to capture a king, if the enemy monarch should happen to be in the path of your rook, your opponent must drop everything else and remove the danger one way or another.

A capture is carried out by moving the rook along the rank or file desired to the square where the enemy piece or pawn resides. Place your rook on that square and remove the enemy piece or pawn from the board.

LONG RANGE

Since the rook can swoop down the entire length or width of the board, it is referred to as a *long-range* piece. But this long-range capability is only good for rooks on an open board—that is, a board without a whole lot of obstacles in the way.

At the start of the game, the rooks are sleeping. None of them have any possible moves, so their power is only a potential for later use. Without open files or ranks the rook is pretty useless, and can get in the way of the other pieces.

OPEN FILES

Open files are files that are free of pawns. Other pieces, both enemy and friendly, can be on the file, and it is still considered open as long as no pawns reside there. A half-open file is a file with at least one enemy pawn on it. Again, pieces of either color can clutter it up, as long as no enemy pawn is in the way.

The Bishop

The tall, thin piece starting out between the royal couple and the knight is an expanded version of the old *alfil*, or "elephant." The bishop is another of the long-range pieces, and it operates on diagonals. So the bishop's strength varies depending in part on what diagonal it stands on.

A bishop on an empty board can move to any square diagonally forward or backward to either side of the square on which it stands. If a piece or pawn stands in the way, however, that's where the bishop must stop. Like rooks, bishops never learned how to jump.

SQUARE COLOR

At the start of a chess game both opponents get two bishops: one dark-square bishop, which is confined to only dark squares for the duration of the game, and one light-square bishop, which is limited to the light squares only. Thus if your light-square bishop gets captured, you might conceivably become weak on the light squares. On the other hand, one of the best ways to begin an attack on the white squares is to remove your opponent's light-square bishop.

FROM ELEPHANT TO BISHOP

The bishop was originally an elephant in the Indian version of chess. It didn't get its modern powers until around the time of the Renaissance. The piece had been a symbol of the elephant's tusks, and that symbol reminded the Italians of a bishop's miter.

CAPTURES

The bishop can capture any piece (except the king) or pawn located on any of its diagonals, provided nothing else is in the way. Simply move the bishop along the desired diagonal, stop at the square the enemy piece or pawn occupies, and remove the offender from the board.

The Queen

The other half of your royal couple is the super-piece of chess. Each side gets only one to begin with, and that's just as well—two would be awfully hard to deal with.

The queen is essentially a rook/bishop combination. She is another long-range piece, like the rook and the bishop, but she combines the power of both. The queens can operate on an empty board along ranks or files, just like a rook, and also along diagonals, just like a bishop. Furthermore, she can operate like both bishops, since in between diagonal moves, she can move along a file or rank and change the color of her diagonal. This is a formidable power.

CAPTURES

The queen can capture just like any chess piece. Sight along the rank, file, or diagonal from where your queen stands, find the piece (excluding the king) or pawn you want to capture, and move the queen there, removing the enemy from the board. Provided nothing is in the way except empty squares, you have made a capture.

TIPS ON USE

The queen is so powerful that most beginning chess players want to bring her out right away to wreak havoc on the enemy position. But this is often a foolish strategy, since the very power of the queen can be turned against her. Any lesser piece or pawn (and in terms of power, by definition that's all of them) can come out and threaten to capture your powerful queen. She will wind up running from one attacker after another while your opponent pours more and more lesser pieces into the fight. It's generally better to hold off on bringing the queen into the attack until the way has been cleared. Then her true power can be unleashed.

The Knight

The peculiar children of chess, knights are shaped like a horse's head and don't behave like any of the other pieces. They do not move along ranks, files, or diagonals. They have a longer range than the king but are not truely long-range like the rook, bishop, or queen. Instead, the knight moves from one corner of any six-square rectangle to the opposite corner. Thus, the rectangular corner highway is what he uses. You will notice very quickly that a knight always winds up on a different color square from where he began his move. Thus in a way he is the bishop's opposite.

CAVALRY TO THE RESCUE

Knights are the cavalry of chess. Although there are no men or horses involved, the jumping action of the rectangular corner leap is close enough to have given players that impression. Along with the king, rook, and pawn, the knight represents one of the original pieces of the earliest Indian and Persian version of chess.

OTHER EXPLANATIONS

The move of the knight is so strange that it takes some getting used to. It has also given rise to a wide variety of explanations. Many chess books introduce it as a piece that moves in an L shape: one square forward along a file, then two squares at a 90° angle along a rank; or two squares to the left along a rank, then one square backward along a file, etc.

Another way of visualizing the knight's move is to think of this piece as a jumper. And as soon as you start to use the knight during a game where many other pieces are in the way, you will see that this is very true. Regardless of whether the squares in the middle of the rectangle are empty or occupied by friendly or enemy pieces, the knight can still make the jump.

THE KNIGHT'S WHEEL

Place a White knight in the center of the board; let's say on d5. Look at all the rectangles that use d5 as one of their corners. Now place a Black pawn on all the opposite corners of those rectangles. You should wind up with a Black pawn on c7, e7, f6, f4, e3, c3, b4, and b6. That is the knight's wheel, which is a great visualizing tool.

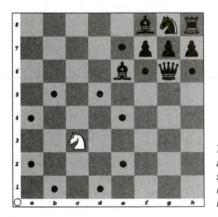

The Black knight can move to any of the three dotted dark squares. The White knight can move to any of the eight dotted light squares.

CAPTURES

Like the other pieces, the knight captures the same way it moves. Spring out from the square the knight occupies, and choose the occupied rectangular corner that is your destination. Land the knight on that square, removing the enemy from the board. You have just completed a knight capture.

Types of Pieces

The five types of pieces can be divided up in several ways. One way is by function:

- King—trapper or trapped; the purpose of the game
- Queen, rook, bishop, and knight—helpers

Another way is by types of move the pieces are capable of. In which case, there are:

- Queen, rook, and bishop—long-range
- King and knight—short-range

Another way to divide up the pieces is by their strength:

- Major pieces—queen and rook
- Minor pieces—bishop and knight

The pieces are assigned a numeric value reflecting their strength. This helps players determine during a game who has an advantage in "material" (the term that refers to captured pieces and pawns). Pawns are worth 1, knights and bishops are worth 3 (generally, though see Chapter 5 for more on piece power), rooks are worth 5, and queens are worth 9 (the king, since it can never be captured, isn't given a numeric value).

You'll notice that the bishop is both a long-range and a minor piece. The reason is that, although its immediate power can be overwhelming, it can only handle half the squares on the chessboard during the life of any game.

The Pawns

These little peasants or foot soldiers are the plodders of chess. They move slowly, one square at a time, and only forward, never backward. In addition, there are many exceptions to the ways they move, making them the toughest guys to master, despite their admitted weakness. It hardly seems worthwhile to put the time and effort into learning the moves!

But the pawn also represents upward mobility and democracy. The pawn is everyman, and each one has the chance to make a difference in the game, if only he survives long enough.

ANY COLOR YOU LIKE

The colors of the pieces can be whatever you like as long as there is clear contrast between the White and Black armies. They don't even have to be white and black; beige and red or cedar and maple are two possible alternatives.

BASIC MOVE

The pawn's basic move is simple enough. Any pawn (each player starts out with eight of them) has the ability to move forward one square along a file or to capture one square forward along a diagonal. The capture is carried out by moving the pawn from its current square to one diagonally forward, removing the enemy piece or pawn there, and taking its place on that square. Right there we have a break from the pattern of the pieces, which move and capture using the same move.

INITIAL TWO-SQUARE ADVANCE

The first time a pawn is used in a game he can move one square forward, as usual, or he can move two squares forward. Thereafter, the option is gone, whether or not it was used. Each pawn has this option whenever he is first moved, regardless of how many moves the game has undergone.

Since the pawn moves forward on a file in this optional move, no capture is possible. The two-squares-forward-along-a-file option is thus there to speed up play, nothing more. (The other exceptions, promotion and en passant, are explained in Chapter 3.)

CHAPTER 2

The Object of the Game

Now that you know the basic moves, it's time to turn to the central question: What are you trying to do in chess?

The answer lies with the king. The king is the whole game, and the object is to place your opponent's king in a position in which he will be captured on the next move. However—and this is very important—every time the king is threatened with capture, he is warned, thus giving him a fighting chance to escape. This warning is called *check*. Winning the game is called *checkmate*.

KING OF KINGS

Like many chess terms, the word *check* comes from Persian. It's derived from the Persian word *shah*, meaning "king." This word is also the origin of the word "chess."

A check is a situation where the king would be in danger of being captured if that were allowed. Instead, the player whose king is in check must drop everything and find a way to get out of check. Any piece or pawn is subject to a similar situation, but no warning is required and the player can ignore the threat to his piece or pawn if he wishes or if he is inattentive.

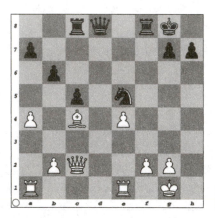

The Black king on g8 is in check from the White bishop on c4.

It sometimes happens that neither player notices a check for several moves. When this is discovered, the players are required to retrace the moves until the king was first in check. It also sometimes happens (in the games of very inexperienced players) that both kings are in check. Such a situation is of course not allowed and the moves must be retraced to a point where only one king is in check.

THREE WAYS OUT OF CHECK
When your king is in check, you must find a way out. There are only three possible ways to get out of check. They are:

1. Capture the attacker.
2. Move the king.

3. Block the attack.

The first way is often the best way. By capturing the piece or pawn delivering the check you not only get out of check so the game can continue, you also remove something valuable to your opponent from the board. Killing two birds with one stone is always good strategy in a game you are trying to win.

The Black king on e8 is in check from the White queen on h5. Get out of check by capturing the queen with the knight on f6.

Black has successfully gotten out of check, picking up a queen in the process.

The second way is the first thing inexperienced players think of, often the only thing. The king is in danger? Move him out of the way. But you must be careful to move the king to a safe square.

The third way works only when your king is in check from a long-range piece with some squares in between the king and the attacking piece. You can block such a check by moving a friendly piece or pawn in the way of the attacker, thus cutting off its long-range power.

The Black king on e8 is in check from the White queen on h5. Block the check by moving the g-pawn to g6.

Black has successfully gotten out of check by blocking the dangerous e8–h5 diagonal with the g-pawn. Note that the g-pawn is now ready to capture the queen in the next move.

SAYING CHECK

When you place your opponent's king in check, you can say "Check" if you wish, but this is not required. If your opponent is experienced, she will realize that her king is in check and will go about trying to find a way out. The check itself is the warning. Actually saying "Check" is a reminder and that reminder is not required.

Checkmate

Just because you have three possible ways to get out of check doesn't mean one of them will always be available. Sometimes only two of the possible ways might be available, or maybe even only one. And what happens if none of the possible solutions happens to present itself? What if you can't get out of check? Then the game is over. Your king is trapped and you lose. This is *checkmate* (often shortened to *mate*).

Checkmate is a position where a king is in check and there is no saving move. Either capturing the checking piece or pawn is not possible or such a capture would leave the king in check anyway. Blocking the check is either impossible or would still leave the king in check from another direction.

THE KING IS HELPLESS

The word *checkmate* may come from the old Persian phrase *shah manad*, meaning "the king is helpless." Some think it comes from *shah mat*, meaning "the king is dead," but how can that be? The king never dies in chess; he is trapped in a checkmate, not killed.

It is not as easy to checkmate a king as it is to capture something else. It isn't enough to simply threaten the king; you also have to make sure there are no ways out.

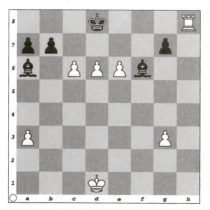

The Black king is checkmated. The rook controls the entire eighth rank, while the pawns control the seventh-rank escape squares.

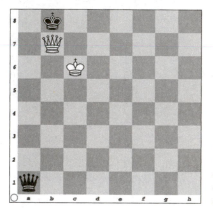

The Black king is checkmated. The White queen checks and controls all the escape squares except her own, b7, which is controlled by the White king.

Winning and Losing

Although checkmate is the goal of a chess game, it is not the only way to end every game. There are at least three other ways to win or lose a game:

- You can win when your opponent runs out of time.
- You can win when your opponent resigns, giving you the game.
- You can win when your opponent fails to show up for a scheduled game, thus forfeiting.

WINNING WITHOUT CHECKMATE

In order to run your opponent out of time you have to be using chess clocks, which we'll discuss later.

The next way to win without checkmate is the most common of all. Most experienced players don't wait for checkmate. They can see it coming, often a long way off. So, rather than fight on in a hopeless situation, they will resign the game, which can be done by offering to shake their opponent's hand or simply saying, "I resign." Another common gesture of resignation is for the resigning player to tip over his king.

Finally, there is the dreaded forfeit. This is an unavoidable consequence of large tournaments; nevertheless, nobody likes them. The winner wins because his opponent didn't show up. The people he advances past with this unearned victory rather resent being beaten out in the standings by someone who didn't play all his games. And the tournament director has to explain it all and try to make this seeming nonsense make sense. But what else can you do when a player shows up for a game and her opponent doesn't? So the forfeit has a place in chess and is here to stay.

HOW NOT TO RESIGN

A great player once jumped up on top of the table, threw his king across the room, and shouted, "Why must I lose to this idiot?" This is not the recommended way of resigning, however. Nor is the unsportsmanlike trick of picking up and leaving the game while your clock is ticking, thus forcing your opponent to wait until your time runs out in order to record his win.

NOBODY WINS OR LOSES

There is another way to end a chess game altogether. It is possible for a chess game to conclude in a draw or a tie, with neither player winning or losing.

There are various ways to "split the point" (draw or tie). These range from the opponents simply agreeing to end hostilities, to various methods outlined in the rules of chess that cover situations where one player may have an advantage but cannot or will not push that advantage through to a checkmate.

POINTS FOR A GAME

In a formal tournament or match, each game is recorded as 1 point for the winner and 0 points for the loser. If the game is a draw, the game is recorded as a ½ point for each player. Thus two draws are equivalent to a win in a tournament or a match.

Draw by Agreement

The simplest form of draw is by agreement. One player offers a draw to his opponent and that player agrees. Anyone can offer a draw at any time during a game, but it is considered bad manners and unsportsmanlike conduct to offer repeatedly after being turned down. During timed games, it is also considered good etiquette to offer a draw on your own time.

When offered a draw, it is considered courteous to at least acknowledge the offer. You might say, "I'll think about it" if you're not ready with an immediate "No!" or "You got it!"

Stalemate

This draw is a strange situation. It ends the game, but there is no check. In a stalemate, there is nothing one of the players can do. Although her king is not in check, any move she makes will expose her king to check, and that is not allowed. So a stalemate ends the game.

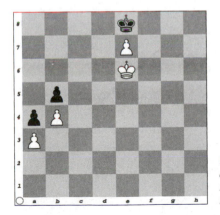

With Black to move, the game ends in stalemate. Black has no legal moves available, and is not in check.

It is a situation that may seem unfair, but that's only if you are the one who put your opponent's king in such an impossible position. Perhaps with such a large advantage you could have found a way to herd that lone king into a corner and checkmate him. Thus, allowing a player with a lone king to escape with a stalemate is often nothing more than carelessness.

On the other hand, if you are the one with the lone king, you might see stalemate as a fantastic opportunity. There have been combinations played where a competitor, sensing trouble, got rid of his remaining pieces in order to bring about a stalemate to end the game in a draw. These types of combinations are available to those who look for them.

So don't disdain stalemate; use it as a weapon. After all, half a point is better than none.

Insufficient Mating Material

Here's a case of a well-thought-out rule. Since nobody can produce a checkmate even if both players cooperate in the demise of one, the game is automatically called a *draw*.

EASY CASES

The simplest case is king against king. Next simplest is king and minor piece against king. These situations are automatic, because the players could play moves until the cows come home and nobody could ever produce a checkmate. Notice that positions with pawns do not qualify. A pawn can "promote" into another piece (how this happens is explained in Chapter 3), so there is always sufficient mating material as long as a single pawn is on the board.

NOT SO EASY

When we get to king and minor piece against king and minor piece, however, we start getting into some trouble. A king and knight cannot checkmate another king and knight, and a king and bishop cannot checkmate another king with a same-colored bishop. But a king and bishop can checkmate a king and knight or a king with an opposite-colored bishop. And a king and knight can checkmate a king and bishop.

All these positions are rather obscure, however. Although checkmates are possible in such positions, they cannot be forced. These checkmates require a cooperative opponent. So for all practical purposes, all such positions are generally abandoned as drawn.

THE LIMITS OF KNIGHTS

A king and two knights cannot force a lone king into submission. Incredible but true. It takes a rook or queen, or two bishops, or a bishop and knight to force a checkmate on a lone king. Or a lowly pawn, who can promote into a rook or queen and thus create enough checkmating material.

Three-Position Repetition

This one is not always completely understood, even by very experienced players. That is because the rule is a bit dry and players have memorized it in a slightly edited form.

THE RULE

In the *U.S. Chess Federation's Official Rules of Chess*, this rule is actually called *Triple occurrence of position*. It runs:

> *The game is drawn upon a correct claim by a player on the move when the same position is about to appear for at least the third time or has just appeared for at least the third time, the same player being on move each time. In both cases, the position is considered the same if pieces of the same kind and color occupy the same squares and if the possible moves of all the pieces are the same, including the right to castle or to capture a pawn en passant.*

POSITION, NOT MOVES

Most players think of this rule as repeating the same move three times consecutively. But you will notice that there is no mention of repeating moves or the same position occurring consecutively.

Most often, this draw comes about by the players repeating moves in order, since that is the easiest way to bring about a repetition of the same position. But it is possible to throw in other moves or to repeat the same position with a different move order, so it's a good idea to know the rule as it is stated in the rulebook.

Here is an example of this triple occurrence of position draw:

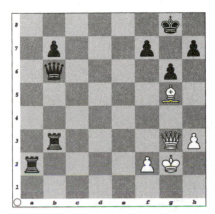

White is in trouble, but the Black king is exposed. So White begins to check. The White queen moves to b8 to check. The Black king moves to g7, and the White queen moves to e5 to check again.

The Black king has to go back to the eighth rank, but he wants to avoid moving to f8, because then the White queen can move to h8 for checkmate. The Black king moves to g8. The White queen then moves to b8 for check. Note that this is the second time this position has occurred.

The Black king then moves to g7. The White queen checks at e5. The Black king escapes to g8 and the White queen again moves to b8 for check.

You no doubt recognize this position by now. It is the third time it has occurred, and the game is therefore drawn.

WHY THE TRIPLE OCCURRENCE DRAW?

The intention of the triple occurrence of position draw is that the players are only wasting time if they keep coming back to the same position. The player who is trying to win must make some sort of progress toward a checkmate, while the player who is trying to draw merely has to keep repeating the position.

Fifty-Move Rule

This rule is intended to prevent players from wasting time by playing random moves that lead nowhere. Under the fifty-move rule, if no pawns are moved and no captures are made in fifty consecutive moves, the game is declared a draw. In this rule, *fifty* is defined as fifty moves by White and fifty moves by Black, so that is still a lot of moves.

In a way this is a very exciting time to be a chess player. It has been hundreds of years since the last big changes in the rules began. Today, thanks to the influence of computers, it is possible we may see another set of rule changes.

CHAPTER 3

En Passant and Other Special Moves

You now know how a chess game is conducted, at least in general, the basic moves of the pieces and pawns, and what you're trying to accomplish. So what's next? Why, all those pesky exceptions to the rules known as *special moves*. There are quite a few, so let's begin.

Touch Move

The rule is simple enough: If you touch a piece or pawn, you must then move that piece or pawn. If you have made a move and let go of whatever piece or pawn you moved, your move is completed.

This rule is sensible and fair—and it is often abused in casual chess. Many players, particularly those who are not very experienced, will notice that something is wrong about a move in the process of making that move or just after making it. Then the temptation to change the move is often hard to resist.

However, it is simply bad manners to change the move in the process of making it, and even poorer manners to change a move that has already been made. Besides, changing the move is against the rules of chess.

J'ADOUBE

There are many foreign terms that have been absorbed into the everyday language of chess, just as foreign terms in music and science have—well, maybe not so many as in science—and in chess, they are treated just like ordinary words. One of these is the French expression *J'adoube*, which means "I adjust." It refers to handling the pieces or pawns prior to making a move when you have no intention of moving that piece or pawn. You may want to do this to adjust the pieces so that they are neater, setting in the center of the squares, or you may simply want to pick up a piece that has fallen down and place it on its proper square.

However, how can your opponent know your intention? If he sees you touch your queen, and he knows that he will win if you move your queen, he may be highly motivated to claim the touch-move rule. But you can circumvent that simply by saying, "J'adoube" (French accent optional) or "I adjust," the English equivalent. That way, everybody knows you had no intention of moving your queen.

J'ADOUBE ETIQUETTE

Say "J'adoube" if you accidentally touch a piece—immediately, if not sooner. If your opponent doesn't hear "J'adoube" or "I adjust," how can she know the touch was accidental?

Promotion

The basic move of the pawn leaves a rather large hole, which I hope you have at least wondered about. What happens when a pawn reaches the far side of the board and there is nowhere else to go? Since a pawn can't move sideways or backward, what use is it?

This is where promotion comes in. Any pawn, upon reaching the farthest possible rank (the eighth rank for White pawns and the first rank for Black pawns) undergoes a metamorphosis. You remove the pawn from the board and replace it with a piece.

Promotion, by the way, has nothing whatsoever to do with any of the pieces already on the board, or even with any of the pieces captured. A pawn upon promoting theoretically turns into whatever piece you want it to turn into (other than a king).

Practically speaking, this doesn't happen, of course. Instead, you must search among captured pieces or get a hold of another set in order to make a second or third queen, for instance. If nothing is available, however, you'll find a way.

A NEW QUEEN

You always have a choice as to which piece you want to turn the pawn into. However, first consider the restrictions: The pawn cannot remain a pawn, and it cannot become a king. Nor can it become an enemy piece (not that you'd even want to make it into one!).

This choice is most often not thought about at all. The queen is such a powerful piece that almost every pawn that is promoted becomes a queen. In fact, this is often called *queening* the pawn.

UNDERPROMOTION

Nevertheless, there are times when you might not want a queen. In these cases, it's good to know that the choice is yours. You can also promote to a rook, a bishop, or a knight. As for why you might want to do such a ridiculous-seeming thing, a very simple example will suffice.

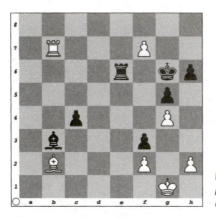

White's pawn is ready to promote. Should it become a queen?

Look at the diagram. You are White and it is your move. If you promote the pawn to a queen, your opponent will then checkmate you (by moving her rook to e1) and you will lose. If, however, you underpromote the pawn to a knight, it is checkmate and you win!

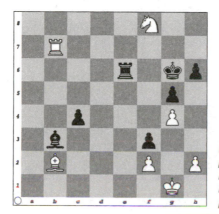

White has decided that greedily promoting to a queen and losing is not the way to go. Underpromotion to a knight produces this checkmate.

Just keep in mind that the choice is yours every time you promote one of your pawns, and your opponent's every time she promotes one of hers.

PROMOTION WITH A CAPTURE

One of the most spectacular changes you can bring about during a chess game is to capture a piece, let's say the opponent's queen, with a pawn while promoting it to a queen. To gain two queens in one move might seem unbelievable, but it is possible.

En Passant

Another French term in general use with chess players is *en passant.* This means "in passing," and it refers to a particular situation that comes up from time to time. It doesn't happen in more than one game in ten, perhaps, but it is a rule you should be aware of if you want to play chess or follow the games of others. To understand en passant, you have to go back to the rule about the pawn's initial two-square option on its first move.

THE SITUATION

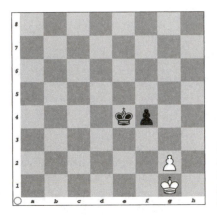

You are playing the White pieces and have a pawn on g2. You have the option of moving that pawn to g3 or g4. Your opponent has a pawn on f4.

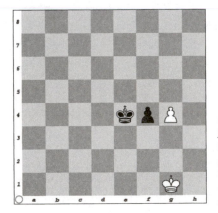

If you move your pawn to g3, your opponent might decide to capture your pawn with her pawn. Therefore, you decide to exercise your two-squares-forward option and move your pawn to g4.

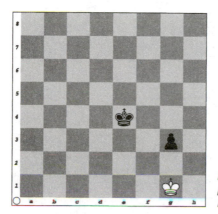

But your opponent captures the pawn on g3, just as if you had moved it there!

This is perfectly legal, and it is a rule you simply have to know about. To repeat, the situation leading up to en passant is:

- A White pawn is on the second rank, unmoved (or a Black pawn is on the seventh rank, unmoved).
- A Black pawn is on an adjacent file on the fourth rank (or a White pawn is on an adjacent file on the fifth rank).
- White exercises the option to move the pawn two squares forward instead of one (or Black exercises the option to move the pawn two squares forward instead of one).
- The Black pawn that was on an adjacent file on the fourth rank captures the White pawn that has just moved two squares forward just as if it had moved only one square forward. (Or the White pawn that was on an adjacent file on the fifth rank captures the Black pawn that has just moved two squares forward just as if it had moved only one square forward.

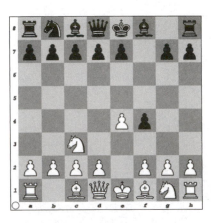

It is White's turn to move, and White decides to move the g-pawn up two squares.

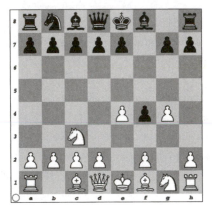

Black can now capture the g4-pawn on g3. Notice that Black cannot capture the e4 pawn.

THE ORIGINS OF EN PASSANT

En passant came to chess during the Renaissance along with the queen and the bishop. It is a natural antidote to the initial two-squares-forward option given to the pawn at the same time. Without en passant, a pawn that has made its way into the opponent's territory would lose some of its power, and opposing pawns could pass by with impunity.

RESTRICTIONS

It is important to remember that an en passant capture can only take place under the specialized conditions just explained. A piece can never capture anything en passant, while a pawn can never capture a piece en passant. In addition, a pawn can never capture another pawn en passant unless that pawn has just exercised its two-squares-forward optional move.

A further restriction on en passant is that the capture has to be executed as a direct response to the two-squares-forward move of the opposing pawn. Wait one move and you lose the option of capturing en passant.

Castling

Unlike en passant, this one comes up often. In practically every game, one player or the other castles or has a chance to castle. Like en passant, castling is a highly restricted move. Certain conditions have to be fulfilled in order to be able to castle.

KING AND ROOK

Before we get into these special conditions, the basic castling move consists of moving both a king and a rook on the same turn. It is the only time in chess that you can move two friendly pieces on the same turn. The king moves two squares along his home rank, while the rook jumps over the king and lands on the opposite side he started from. Both moves are impossible separately, since kings normally move only one square in any direction while rooks normally don't jump over anything, needing a clear file or rank in order to move at all.

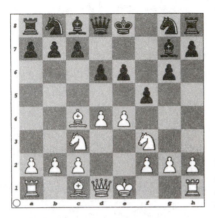

White's king and h1 rook have not moved. There is nothing in between the two except empty squares.

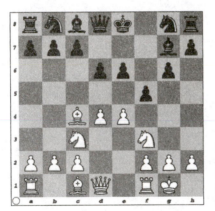

White has moved the king two squares to the right along the first rank and jumped the rook over the king to its other side. Castling is completed.

Castling serves two purposes. One is to tuck the vulnerable king away in a corner for safety during the early part of the game. Opposing pieces may be flying around the middle of the board, and staying there may not be healthy for the valuable king. The other purpose is to allow the rook to get involved in the action through the middle of the board. This is usually much better than moving the rook up the h- or a-file along the edge of the board.

CONDITIONS

In order for castling to occur, the following conditions have to be present:

- The squares between king and rook must be empty.
- Both king and rook must be on their original squares.
- Both king and rook must not have been moved (since the beginning of the game).
- The king cannot castle into check.
- The king cannot castle out of check. (Remember, the three ways out of check did not include castling.)
- The king cannot castle through check.

That last restriction is a little tricky. It means that the king can't pass over any square that is directly under control of an enemy piece. For example, a White king on e1 and a White rook on h1 are ready to castle, as long as neither has moved, the king is not in check, and the f1 and g1 squares are empty. But if there is a Black bishop on d3, which controls the f1 square, castling is not possible.

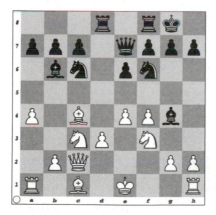

White cannot castle because the king would wind up on g1, in check from the b6 bishop.

WHERE DOES CASTLING COME FROM?

Castling is the newest move in chess. It has only been standardized within the last 150 years. Before that there were many ways to castle, including the king and rook actually trading places or completing it in two separate moves, with the king moving first and the rook jumping over him on the next move.

KINGSIDE AND QUEENSIDE

There are two types of castling, depending on the direction in which you decide to castle. In kingside castling, the White king goes to g1 while the White h1 rook goes to f1. (The Black king goes to g8 while the Black h8 rook goes to f8.) The kingside is simply the half of the board where the kings start out. Thus, kingside refers to the e-, f-, g-, and h-files.

In queenside castling, the king goes in the other direction. The queenside is that half of the board where the queens start out. Thus queenside refers to the d-, c-, b-, and a-files. The White king goes to c1 and the White rook on a1 goes to d1. (The Black king goes to c8 while the Black rook on a8 goes to d8.)

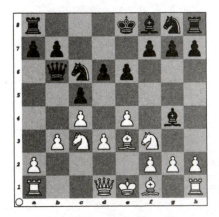

Black's king and a8 rook have not moved. There is nothing in between the two except empty squares.

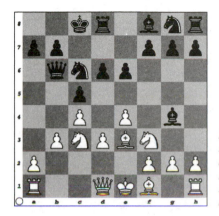

Black has moved the king two squares to the left along the eighth rank and jumped the rook over the king to its other side. Queenside castling is completed.

The restrictions about castling out of, into, and through check apply only to the king. If your rook is under attack from an enemy piece but your king is safe on its starting square, and would be safe on the square it passes over as well as the square it lands on in the process of castling, castling is legal.

You will notice that in queenside castling there is an extra file to take into account. The king always moves two squares to the side when castling, so it is the rook that has to travel further in queenside castling.

ONLY ONCE

A particularly important restriction to castling is that it can only be done once in a game by each player. This is inherent in the castling rules, since castling cannot take place unless the king and the rook he castles with are unmoved. Thus once you castle, that condition can no longer be met for the rest of the game.

The Clock

We've covered all the special moves in chess as long as you don't consider the chess clock. But clocks are often used to time games, whether in tournaments or in clubs or just to make a friendly game in somebody's home, in a park, or on the Internet move quickly.

A chess clock is really two clocks in one housing. Once you make a move, you press the button on your clock and it will stop ticking while your opponent's clock will begin ticking. Once your opponent makes his move and presses the button on his clock, your clock will start ticking while his stops. That way the entire game can be timed, with each player only being charged for the time it takes to come up with a move.

Chess clocks come in two types. A digital chess clock is one that displays the exact number of minutes and seconds available for each player. When a player runs out of time using a digital clock, the display reads "00:00." A mechanical clock (sometimes referred to as *analog*) is one with the traditional clock face and hands. A mechanical clock also has a device called a *flag* that signals when a player's time has expired. When a player runs short of time using a mechanical clock, the hands of the clock begin to raise the player's flag. When time expires, the player's flag falls.

SPEED OR RAPID CHESS

Chess players often want to play a great number of games very quickly. There are various reasons for this, but we'll just look at how to do it. First, you need a chess clock. You set the clock for five minutes for each player (or seven minutes, three minutes, or whatever you want) and commence playing. Each player must make all of his or her moves in the allotted time of five minutes (or whatever is agreed upon). If the agreed-upon time is five minutes, the game will last no longer than a total of ten minutes.

As long as the players remember to push in the button on their side of the clock, the game will move along until someone plays a checkmate or gets one of various drawn positions or until somebody's flag falls. If that happens, that person has run out of time and automatically loses, just as if he had been checkmated.

BULLET PLAY

A variation on speed play is the bullet chess so popular on the Internet. That usually allows one minute for the game by each player. Of course, you don't use a separate clock for such chess, since the clock is automatic, and your move triggers the change of time from you to your opponent and back again.

SLOWER TIME LIMITS

Yet another way to use a chess clock is to give each player a set amount of time for a set amount of moves. A very popular time limit used to be forty moves in two hours. In this version of timed chess, the players must keep score if they want to be able to make a claim that their opponent overstepped the time limit. Otherwise, how could anybody know when forty moves were reached? In this type of play, keeping track of the moves is an essential ingredient. You will learn more about keeping score of a game in Chapter 4.

FURTHER RULES

New rules have been made to accommodate players who are easily winning the position (that is, given the position of the pieces on the board, they have a reasonably clear path to victory) but have no time to play out the win. These rules cover lack of mating material, insufficient losing chances, and a new device on chess clocks known as *time increments*. They're all there waiting for you should you decide to get involved in tournament chess.

CHAPTER 4

Notation—Keeping Track of Your Game

Chess notation is probably as old as chess. It is nothing more than a way to record positions, problems, and combinations so that they can be reproduced. Such notation provides a way to read and write chess, so a record can be kept of any game.

Why Keep Records?

There are many reasons for keeping a record of a chess game. Unless you have a fantastic memory, keeping score of a game is the best way to make the moves available for critique afterward. This is one of the best ways to improve your game, whether the critique is done by you alone, you with your opponent (better), or you and your opponent along with a third party, perhaps an experienced player (best).

THE CHESS WORLD

Knowing how to read a game score brings the entire world of chess into your home. There are newspaper columns, chess magazines, and a fantastically huge number of chess books on the market. Chess masters have been writing down their thoughts, analyses, and systems for hundreds of years. This is all open to one who knows how to read chess notation and opaque to one who does not.

Chess-playing computers, chess-playing software programs, huge chess databases, and chess Web pages all use chess notation. You're missing out on an awful lot if you don't know how to read chess.

If you ever decide that you want to improve at chess, you will need to know chess notation. Whether you want to get good enough to beat the computer or someone in particular, or to gain a national or international title or rating, you simply cannot progress without it. No coach or teacher will be able to help you much if you don't have game scores to work with, and you won't even be able to scrutinize your own games without this knowledge.

BLINDFOLD CHESS

Blindfold chess, and especially simultaneous blindfold chess, can be accomplished only by those who understand chess notation. The chess master, who has no set or board in sight, calls out her moves. The opponent or opponents, who have sets and boards in front of them and can see the game in progress, call out a response.

WIN ON TIME

You win if your opponent runs out of the allotted time before making the prescribed number of moves in a tournament game. The only way to show that this has indeed happened, though, is to have your game score ready along with the clock that shows the time is up. Obviously this cannot be done unless you have kept a record of the game.

Correspondence and e-mail games are not possible without chess notation. For that matter, chess played over the telephone and blindfold chess are also prohibitively difficult without a notation system.

THE LIBRARY OF CHESS

There have been more books written about chess than about all other games combined. The game has a wide appeal, and its language is understood all over the world. Knowing the language of chess can put you in touch with people from every corner of the globe.

You Already Know the Basics!

After having just learned how widespread chess is, would it be a surprise to learn that you already know the basics of chess notation? Well, prepare to be surprised, because you already do!

You already know what each square is called, after all, and you know the names of every rank and file and diagonal on the board. In addition, you know the names of all the chess pieces and pawns and the names of their special moves. You also know about check, checkmate, and stalemate.

BATTLESHIP

Have you ever played Battleship? That's the game where you hide your ships on a grid and try to destroy the ships of your opponent on his grid by calling out coordinates. The grids aren't checkered, but the grid coordinates are none other than chess square coordinates: e1, g2, h4, a7, etc. All right, so there are a few other things to know about chess notation, but again, you are already familiar with everything here.

RECORDING YOUR OPINION

You can record your opinion about a move of a chess game very succinctly: Just use punctuation. The following table of punctuation marks that follow moves is understood all over the world. Whenever you see such punctuation after a move, you know that it is the opinion of the annotator (the one writing about the game).

PUNCTUATION MARK	MEANING
!	A very good or surprising move
!!	A particularly strong and surprising move
?	A weak move
??	A blunder; giving something away
!?	An interesting move
?!	A dubious move that has some strong points

SPECIFICS

Pieces are designated by capital letters: K is for king, Q is for queen, R is for rook, B is for bishop, and N is for knight (since K is reserved for the king). The pawn has no symbol. It used to be P, but that has been done away with in the interest of simplicity.

A move is written as the symbol of the piece being moved followed by the square that piece lands on. A capture is indicated by an **x** between the piece symbol and the square on which the capture takes place. Check is indicated by a + after the move, and checkmate is indicated by a # after the move that produces it. Stalemate is handled by writing ½–½.

Any ambiguities (such as when you have a rook on a1 and a rook on h1 and nothing in between, and want to move one of your rooks to d1) are handled by simply adding an extra identifying letter or number. In the case just cited, **Rad1** or **Rhd1** will convey your meaning precisely.

Keep in mind that all square names and file symbols contain lowercase letters only. Capital letters are reserved for the piece symbols.

HOW TO NOTE A CASTLE

Castling is indicated in chess notation by the use of zeros to indicate the number of squares between the king and rook, separated by a hyphen. Thus castling kingside looks like **0-0**, while castling queenside looks like **0-0-0**.

MOVE NUMBERS

The moves are all numbered, beginning with the first move, which is move 1, and the next move, which is move 2, etc. Each numbered move includes White's turn and Black's turn. Since White moves first in a game, his move is always given first, and Black's is given next.

ELLIPSES

In notation, you'll sometimes see an ellipsis (. . .). This is an indication that the annotator has left out half the move. For instance, 11. . . d4 means that in the eleventh move of the game, Black moved a pawn to the d4 square. White's move was left out by the annotator either because he'd already previous indicated what it was or because it wasn't essential to what he was saying.

PAWN MOVES

Just like the movement of the pawn, the notation for pawn moves is different. When a pawn moves, it is written simply as the destination square. You might expect a typical first move to be written **Pe4**, but actually it is the simpler **e4**. When pawns capture, the notation is the file letter followed by an **x** for a capture, followed by the destination square (**dxe5**). When a pawn promotes, it is written as the move followed by an equal sign followed by the symbol for the piece the pawn has promoted to (**d8=Q** or **hxg8=N+**).

An entire game can thus be described in a single paragraph. Get out a chessboard, set up the pieces for the start of a game, and then play through the following game:

1. e4 e5 2. Nf3 d6 3. d4 Bg4 4. dxe5 Bxf3 5. Qxf3 dxe5 6. Bc4 Nf6 7. Qb3 Qe7 8. Nc3 c6 9. Bg5 b5 10. Nxb5 cxb5 11. Bxb5+ Nbd7 12. 0-0-0 Rd8 13. Rxd7 Rxd7 14. Rd1 Qe6 15. Bxd7+ Nxd7 16. Qb8+ Nxb8 17. Rd8#.

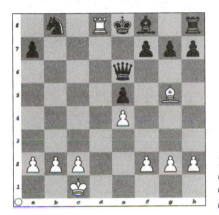

This is the final position. If you have come up with something else, go back and make sure you play all the moves correctly.

Algebraic Notation

What you have just read through is a game written in algebraic notation. There are other forms of algebraic notation besides the forms you have just learned about. There is *long form*, where the square the piece or pawn comes from is recorded as well as the square it goes to, like this: **1. e2-e4 e7-e5 2. Ng1-f3 d7-d6 3. d2-d4 Bc8-g4 4. d4xe5 Bg4xf3**, etc. Then there is *short form*, which dispenses with anything unnecessary. Even the capture sign is done away with, since playing through the game makes the capture obligatory anyway: **1. e4 e5 2. Nf3 d6 3. d4 Bg4 4. de Bf3**, etc.

ENGLISH DESCRIPTIVE NOTATION

In the old English descriptive notation, the files are given the names of the pieces that occupy the first square on them in the original position. To distinguish the two sides of the board from one another (right vs. left), those pieces near the king are known as KR (king's rook), KN (king's knight), and KB (king's bishop). Similarly, those nearest the queen are known as QR (queen's rook), QN (queen's knight), and QB (queen's bishop).

The eight files with their descriptions are identical for White and Black. The ranks are numbered from 1 to 8, with each player beginning from his or her own side, so that "1" for White is "8" for Black. In this way, each square carries a unique letter and a number, making it easy to determine which piece is being moved from square to square. It's this unique "addressing" that allows moves to be accurately recorded.

In English descriptive, captures are handled differently and the pawn gets the symbol P. Also, the symbol for check is ch rather than +, and a checkmate is ++ or written out.

Here is the same game you just looked at, written in English descriptive notation:

1. P-K4 P-K4 2. N-KB3 P-Q3 3. P-Q4 B-N5 4. PxP BxN 5. QxB PxP 6. B-QB4 N-KB3 7. Q-QN3 Q-K2 8. N-B3 P-B3 9. B-KN5 P-N4 10. NxP PxN 11. BxPch QN-Q2 12. 0-0-0 R-Q1 13. RxN RxN 14. R-Q1 Q-K3 15. BxRch NxB 16. Q-N8ch NxQ 17. R-Q8 checkmate.

THE LIMITS OF DESCRIPTIVE NOTATION

Descriptive notation used to be popular in many countries, but it is more complex than algebraic notation and isn't universal. Many of the old classic chess books written in descriptive notation have since been translated into algebraic notation.

Other Notations

There are other notation systems you may come across from time to time. Spanish descriptive, Russian descriptive, and German descriptive are all very similar to English descriptive, except that the piece symbols correspond to the names of the pieces in those languages.

There is a special international correspondence notation system that is the simplest of all: Each square is assigned two numbers (both ranks and files are numbered) and moves are described as the square a piece or pawn has vacated and the square it moves to.

FORSYTH NOTATION

There are notation systems for describing a chess position without bothering with the moves that led up to it. One such is Forsyth notation, in which each White piece or pawn is given as a capital letter and each Black piece or pawn as a lowercase letter. Empty squares are indicated by a number according to how many empty squares there are.

Forsyth positions are set up like a diagram, with the White pieces at the bottom and the Black pieces at the top. Each row consists of a rank, starting with the eighth rank and continuing down to the first rank.

The final checkmate in the game we have been discussing looks like this in Forsyth notation:

1n1Rkb1r

p4ppp

4q3

4p1B1

4P3

8

PPP2PPP

2K5

ANOTHER POSITION NOTATION

Of course, it's just as easy to simply describe the pieces that are on the board and the squares they are on. Again, describing the same checkmate position:

Black: Ke8, Qe6, Rh8, Bf8, Nb8, Pa7, e5, f7, g7, h7

White: Kc1, Rd8, Bg5, Pa2, b2, c2, e4, f2, g2, h2

BRAILLE NOTATION

There is one other type of chess notation: Braille. Blind people can and do play chess. They don't play "blindfold," however, like a master at an exhibition. Instead, they use special boards and pieces that they are allowed to touch at all times, since their fingers are their eyes. They record and read chess games in Braille notation.

Diagrams

These notation systems for positions are all right as far as they go. But they won't be of much help unless you have a chessboard and set so that you can display a position. That is, unless you can easily visualize a position from the description. Not many people can do that readily.

So printed diagrams have come into use. These diagrams are simply a small picture of a chessboard with the pieces and pawns shown on their correct squares. You have already been making use of diagrams throughout this book, and will continue doing so.

Making diagrams is simply a matter of squishing a three-dimensional board with pieces and pawns into two dimensions. It's accomplished by picturing the board as if as seen from above, and the pieces as simple symbols of the actual pieces.

PROBLEMS

Diagrams are also useful in showing problems for the student or interested reader to solve. These include positions from games where a combination will bring about a dramatic change. They also include composed problems where the solver is asked to find a checkmate in a specified number of moves. Other composed problems will ask the solver to find a winning series of moves.

Game Scores

There are score sheets and score pads available at any tournament and for sale in stores and through the United States Chess Federation. You can use these to write down a game in progress.

The score will look somewhat different from those you see in magazines and books, but this is only because score sheets line up the moves in neat columns, rather than spreading them out in a paragraph.

COLLECTIBLES

One of the most famous and exciting games in chess history was played on October 17, 1956. The players were Donald Byrne, an international master, and thirteen-year-old Bobby Fischer, then beginning his triumphant ascent in the chess world. Fischer, playing Black, defeated Byrne by, among other things, dramatically sacrificing his queen. Fischer's tournament sheet on which he recorded his moves for what one commentator called the "Game of the Century" (not to be confused with Fischer's later "Match of the Century" against Boris Spassky) was purchased by a fan and later resold and resold again. It's estimated that were it to be sold today, it would bring more than $100,000.

In a typical score sheet, there will be two sets of numbered columns for a total number of four columns. The left-hand column is for White's moves. The next column to the right is for Black's moves. The third column is for later White moves. They are numbered, continuing from the bottom of the first column. The last column is for later Black moves.

PART II

BEATING YOUR OPPONENT

CHAPTER 5

The Basics of Strategy in a Chess Game

Now that you know how to play chess, and how to read and write chess, it is time to learn how to play with a reasonable degree of skill. This will also allow you to appreciate the skill and artistry of the masters. Anything beyond that is subject to talent and/or lots of structured work and play.

Principles to Follow

Before getting into the specifics of good play, we'll begin with a few general principles to follow during a game. These will help you in determining what move or plan to choose.

- The safety of both kings is the first priority.
- Greater force generally defeats lesser force.
- Control the center and you control the game.

- Control more squares and your opponent is smothered.
- Develop your pieces early and often.
- Long-range pieces need open lines to function well.
- Healthy pawns mean a healthy game.
- Whenever possible, operate with threats.

These are enough to start with. So let's look at them one at a time.

King Safety

The primacy of king safety is inherent in the rules. If your king is not safe, he may become trapped, and that means you lose. At the same time, you cannot win if your opponent's king remains safe. You must do something to trap the enemy monarch in order to win. So this principle is double-edged. It gives you a hint of what to keep in mind at all times during a chess game.

YOUR KING

The first part of the principle implies safety for your own king. So the question becomes, "How do I make my king safe?" At the start of the game, he is surrounded by a queen, a bishop, and three pawns. Your king is in no immediate danger there.

The trouble starts with the other part of the principle. You begin the game by getting your pieces ready for an assault on the enemy king. But to do that, at least some of your pieces and pawns must necessarily leave the side of your own king. When that happens, he is no longer as safe as he was at the start of the game.

CASTLING

One of the best ways to ensure king safety is to tuck your big guy in a corner by way of castling. With three pawns in front of him and a rook by his side, and often a knight or even a bishop in the vicinity as well, your king has a good chance of maintaining reasonable safety for some time.

Later in the game, this fortress may be broken down and your king may have to leave. But as long as you make sure that doesn't occur until a number of pieces have been exchanged via capturing, you should be all right.

BRINGING OUT THE KING

The king often comes out boldly later in the game. When the danger of checkmate is reduced because the enemy doesn't have many pieces (because a number have been captured), you can use your king as an added attacking force. Just make sure the danger of checkmate is really significantly reduced!

THE OTHER KING

The other part of the first principle is the enemy king. You generally can't win the game if you can't checkmate him. But, of course, most opponents are going to be very annoying about not letting you near their royal leader.

Against a reasonably skilled opponent, you will not be able to put together a quick checkmating attack. So you have to build up your attack, using the other principles to gather your forces for the final blow.

Meanwhile, you have to keep in mind the final target as well as your own king's defense. It's a delicate balance, and you'll be confronted with it throughout any given game.

THE FASTEST CHECKMATE

Perhaps you are wondering what is the fastest checkmate. It is referred to as the fool's mate, and it takes a total of two moves! The fool plays White, and the game goes **1. f4 e6 2. g4 Qh4#**.

It takes a little longer for a fool to lose playing Black: **1. e4 e5 2. Qh5 Ke7 3. Qxe5#**.

Another fast checkmate is called scholar's mate: **1. e4 e5 2. Bc4 Nc6 3. Qh5 Nf6 4. Qxf7#**.

Greater Force

Look at the previous checkmates and you can easily see what is meant by greater force. In all of them, the poor king got clobbered by an enemy queen. In the first two, the fool opened up lines of attack for the enemy and closed off all retreat or blocking opportunities.

In the third checkmate, the triumphant queen swooped in with the help of a friendly bishop.

PIECE POWER

In Chapter 1 you learned the relative strength of the pawns and pieces as expressed by a numeric value, but judging the power of each piece is a bit more complicated. In order to compare them, we need a measuring stick. So let's take the least powerful of all, the pawn, and use that as our measure. Here are all the pieces listed in terms of their average power, expressed in terms of numbers of pawns:

- Knight = 3½
- Bishop = 3½
- Rook = 5
- Queen = 9
- King = infinity

There are several things about this list that may appear surprising or obscure. For instance, how can anything be worth half a pawn? And what is that about infinity?

A rook is generally stronger than a minor piece (a bishop or a knight). This difference is worth about 1½ pawns, and is called the *Exchange*. This is not to be confused with the general term *exchange*, which refers to trading one piece for another—that is, capturing an enemy piece of the same value as one which you have lost to the enemy. Thus you can exchange bishops, or exchange a queen for a rook and knight, but if you trade a rook for a knight you have given up the Exchange.

UNEQUAL BALANCE

Sometimes this list is represented with the bishops and knights being worth only 3 pawns. This is not so far wrong, but we get messed up when we take three minor pieces and compare them to the queen. Together, they are significantly stronger than her majesty. And a bishop and knight are generally a bit stronger than a rook and pawn. So the half-pawns are there to make it all come out a bit better.

It's hard to compare bishops and knights; they are so different. Knights can cover the entire board eventually, while bishops can cover only half the squares. Yet bishops are long-range pieces and have a lot more immediate power than any knight.

Sometimes a bishop is better, and sometimes a knight is better. But when you fight with two bishops against two knights or against a bishop and a knight, it is usually better to have the bishops. Together they have long-range power *and* can cover every square on the board.

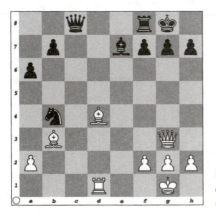

White is poised to checkmate on g7. Note the power of both bishops.

It's almost unfair to have this much power.

KING EQUAL TO INFINITY

But what about the king being equal to infinity? That is in the very nature of chess. You can't put a value on the king, since he is not subject to capture. Thus all the pieces and pawns together won't equal his importance. As for his power when there are not many pieces left later in a game, it is something on the order of 4 pawns.

GREATER FORCE GENERALLY WINS

Greater force generally wins against lesser force. But only generally. In a sacrifice, a player gives up some greater force in order to bring about a concentration of force in a particular area of the board.

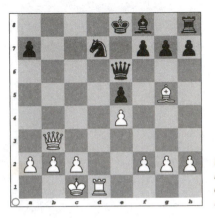

White plays 16. Qb8+! 17. NXb8 Rd8 checkmate. The sacrifice of the queen paves the way for mate.

AVERAGE POWER

It is important to remember that these measurements are averages only. Rooks are generally much stronger than pawns, but what about a pawn about to promote to a queen? Bishops are about equal with knights, but what about a bishop locked behind its own pawns with nowhere to go, compared with a knight that can hop over the whole board with impunity?

You can think of each piece and its average power as a potential. As long as you keep this in mind, you won't go too far wrong when exchanging a piece for a supposedly less powerful piece that is doing a lot of damage.

Chess has good bishops and bad bishops. A good bishop is one with open diagonals, many places to go, and pieces and pawns to annoy.

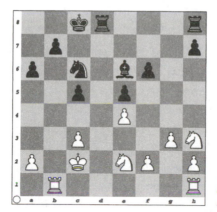

The bishop gives White headaches on both sides of the board (a2 and h3).

A bad bishop is one that is trapped behind its own pawns. It doesn't have anything reasonable to do, and is sometimes referred to as a *tall pawn*, though sometimes even a pawn would be better. At least a pawn can move one square forward on a file.

The bishop has nowhere to go, and blocks the B8 rook as well.

Control the Center

The importance of controlling the central squares is easy to illustrate. Just take an empty board and place a knight on the corner. Count up the number of squares it can jump to. The number is two.

Now place the knight somewhere along the middle of an edge of the board. You will find three or four possible squares for the knight now. That's twice the power.

Next, place the knight on one of the central squares. You will now see eight possible destinations for the knight. In other words, the knight has four times as much power in the center than it had on the edge of the board.

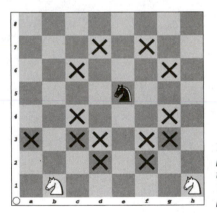

The h1 knight has minimal power. The b1 knight has about twice as many moves available. The e5 knight is about twice as powerful as the b1 knight.

Try the bishop next. The results aren't as dramatic, but you will notice that the bishop gains in power from controlling seven squares to controlling thirteen squares.

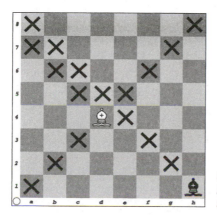

Compare the power of the bishops and see why it's better to control central squares.

ROOKS FRONT AND CENTER!

On an empty board, the rook seems to be just as powerful anywhere you place it. But that's not quite true. It can travel in four directions anywhere on the board except along the a-file, h-file, first rank, or eighth rank—in other words, the edge of the board. So even the rook is stronger in the center.

BUSY METROPOLIS

The roads themselves are oriented toward the center, which we explored briefly in Chapter 2. Since there are more squares to visit from the center than from anywhere else, it shouldn't be too much of a surprise that the pieces are actually stronger in the center than they are anywhere else.

You can think of the chessboard as a hill, with the center being the highest elevation, and the outer squares being the lowest. Viewed in this way, chess becomes very like a case of king of the hill.

COUNTERATTACK IN THE CENTER

An attack on the flank, or side of the board, is best met by a counterattack in the center. This is true even if the object of attack is your king. The point is that an attack against your king on the side of the board won't work unless your opponent can bring up reinforcements through the center.

HEALTHY PIECES

Think back to the table of piece power in terms of pawns. It should be clear by now why this table is only an average. Certainly a knight on e4 and a knight on a1 do not have the same power. As the game progresses, some pieces gain in power as they occupy the center or control it from afar, while others suffer from a lack of good, healthy central air. There are other ways in which pieces gain and lose power during a game, but always keep in mind that they are generally strongest in or close to the center.

THE VALUE OF CENTER PAWNS

Even the lowly pawn benefits from being in the center. From here, a pawn can keep unwanted enemy pieces out. A pawn on the a-file or h-file just doesn't have the same power. There is only one direction in which to capture instead of the normal two.

Control More Squares

This one is already familiar. Since there are sixty-four squares on the board, take control of thirty-three, or more than half of them, and you will begin to smother your opponent. A smothered opponent is said to have a *cramped* game. There is a principle of strategy covering such a situation that is very useful to know. It comes in the following two parts.

WHEN CRAMPED, EXCHANGE PIECES

Since having a cramped position restricts your possible moves, your pieces do not operate at their most efficient level. A great way to fight out of such a situation is to exchange pieces.

You don't need anything fancy here. Just trade your minor pieces for your opponent's minor pieces and your rooks for your opponent's rooks. This gives your remaining pieces more room to breathe.

Black to move relieves the cramp by exchanging: 1. ... Nxd4 2. Qxd4 Bxb5 3. Nxb5.

WHEN CONTROLLING SPACE, AVOID EXCHANGES

The other side of this principle is that when you control more squares than your opponent, avoid piece exchanges. This ensures your opponent will never get rid of all those cumbersome cramped pieces that step all over each other's toes.

Develop the Pieces

Playing a chess game is similar to coaching a sports team. You don't actually expose yourself to physical injury, but you do decide what your players will do. Your team in chess is not made of people, however. Rather, it is made of pieces and pawns.

TEAM SPORT

So think of a team sport. Anything you prefer will do: football, soccer, hockey, or basketball. Any sport that pits a group of players against another group of players will be appropriate.

Let's take basketball for example. You are sending five players against the enemy five to score more points. So what do you think of this strategy: Send your best scorer out against the other team while the rest of your players watch the action?

It doesn't take a genius to figure out that such a strategy will not work very well. In fact, it's so bad, no coach would even think of trying it. Yet that is the very strategy many inexperienced chess players go for after learning of the tremendous power of the queen. Yes, she is strong, but she cannot do it all herself. Instead, you need to *develop* other pieces—that is, send them out from their starting positions so they can begin executing your battle plan.

A famous case of a player with a big lead in development (and, incidentally, controlling the center) carrying out a successful attack is Legal's mate. This trap is named after De Kermur, Sire de Légal, a strong eighteenth-century player.

1. e4 e5 2. Nf3 d6 3. Bc4 Bg4 4. Nc3 g6.

Black has moved only pawns and now brings out a bishop where it is undefended. White has developed and played to control the center.

5. Nxe5! Bxd1 6. Bxf7+ Ke7 7. Nd5#.

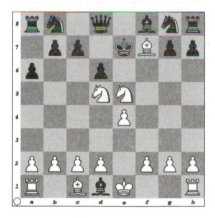

Three minor pieces and a pawn control the center and thus the exposed Black king.

BUILD UP POWER

Since greater force generally defeats lesser force, and since you cannot gain greater force immediately against an experienced opponent, you will need to build up your force gradually. The way to do that is to develop a new piece with each move.

The trouble with the losing strategy in Legal's mate is that Black only developed one piece during the entire game: The bishop moved to g4 and captured a queen. All the rest of Black's moves involved pushing pawns or getting the king out of check.

Meanwhile, White developed first a knight, then a bishop, and then another knight, and finally began a powerful attack using those pieces and his control of the center. It's a clear case of what in basketball they call a three-on-one break.

MOVING THE SAME PIECE AGAIN

A very good principle to keep in mind in chess is to move a different piece each time it is your move unless there is a particularly strong reason to move one you have already brought out. Then your problem becomes one of recognizing those strong reasons when they come up. They include:

- You will lose a piece or pawn if you don't move a developed piece.
- You can begin a winning attack by moving a developed piece.
- You can force your opponent to abandon his plan of attack by making a threat with a developed piece.
- There are no undeveloped pieces left to move.

A very good short-term goal to shoot for in the early part of the game is connecting your rooks. That means to empty out the squares between your rooks on the first rank if you are White or on the eighth rank if you are Black. You can begin this by bringing out your minor pieces so that they control the central squares. Next, you can castle. That will connect your rooks and leave your king safe.

Both sides have developed pieces and castled.

Developing pieces means not just getting them off their original positions. It also means putting them where they will do some good. So you need to have a pretty good idea where that will be.

Long-Range Pieces Need Open Lines

Bishops, rooks, and queens won't ever do you any good unless they can oversee open lines. Any that sit behind friendly pawns represent unused potential. The thing to remember is that the bishops can come out into the melee early, while it is generally a good idea to hold back a bit on bringing out the rooks and queens.

The reason is simple. Bishops are less valuable than the major pieces, so they can be exposed earlier. Also, rooks are a bit awkward when there are many pieces and pawns crowding the board. They are at their best later in the game when many pieces have been exchanged. The more ranks and files open up for them, the better off they are.

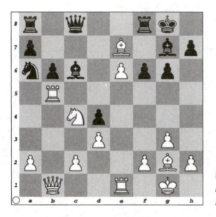

White to move. Look at the White long-range pieces and note how many squares they control.

FIANCHETTO

Fianchetto, which derives from an Italian word meaning "flank," refers to the development of a bishop at g2, b2, b7, or g7. These squares are near the side of the board, but from them, the bishop commands one of the longest diagonals. Fianchettoed bishops control the center from the side of the board.

The problem with a fianchetto development is that an extra pawn move has to be made to make room for the bishop. This can cause problems, particularly if your king is nearby after castling.

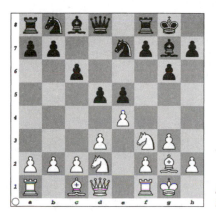

Both sides have fianchettoed their bishops on the kingside

KNIGHTS NEED OUTPOSTS

An *outpost* is a square in or near the center that is protected by a friendly pawn. This is an ideal square for a short-hopping knight. Even better is a *hole*, which is an outpost in the opponent's territory that cannot be assailed by an enemy pawn.

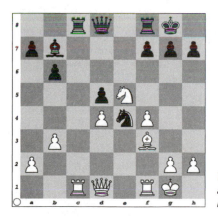

The knight on e5 is occupying an outpost. The knight on e4 is in a hole.

Keep in mind that minor pieces, and major pieces as well, need secure squares in order to function properly. If your opponent can drive your piece away from its open file, diagonal, or outpost with a pawn, or by attacking where it cannot be defended, your piece is not secure.

Healthy and Unhealthy Pawns

So far the pieces have been the subject of discussion. But now we come to the pawns. As usual, they have to be handled differently in coming up with a viable strategy. The difference between pawns and pieces is that pawns have to be considered in groups. And each grouping has to be handled differently. Here are the main pawn groups:

- Pawn phalanx
- Pawn chain
- Doubled pawn
- Isolated pawn
- Passed pawn

PAWN PHALANX

A *pawn phalanx* is a group of two or more pawns on the same rank, on adjacent files. This formation is strong, particularly in the center or in your opponent's territory, because they control the row of squares directly in front of them. This keeps enemy pieces out.

White has a mighty pawn phalanx with his d-, e-, and f-pawns. Black has defensive pawn phalanxes on the a- and b-files and on the d- and e-files.

This formation can be vulnerable from the side or rear, just as any pawn is. So if you control those squares, you have a powerful weapon. A great strategy when playing against a pawn phalanx is to force one of the pawns to move forward or capture something, thus breaking up the phalanx. A good way to break up an enemy pawn phalanx is to attack it with your own pawns.

PHALANX TO CHAIN

If one of the pawns in a phalanx moves forward, we no longer have a phalanx. We then have a pawn chain.

PAWN CHAIN

One pawn defending another along a forward-looking diagonal is a *pawn chain*. There can be chains of four or five pawns lined up like this, each pawn defending the one in front.

The front pawn or pawns in a chain are strong. Capture one and you can expect a recapture from the pawn behind. But a pawn chain has a weakness. The base of the chain, or the pawn behind it all that supports the entire chain, can be vulnerable. So the best strategy when operating against a pawn chain is to attack the base of the chain. If the supporting pawn falls, the entire chain may crumble.

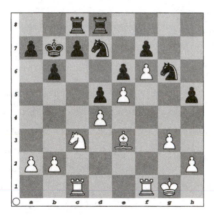

Black's move should be 1. ... c5!, striking at d4, the base of White's pawn chain.

DOUBLED PAWN

A *doubled pawn* is a group of two friendly pawns on the same file. They can be strong along the adjacent files, since enemy pieces will find the squares there to be unsafe. But they are almost useless as attackers. The square directly in front of the doubled pawns is vulnerable to control by the enemy, and they cannot form phalanxes unless allowed to capture something.

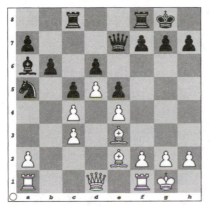

White's c-pawns are doubled.

One byproduct of doubled pawns is the open file produced when making the capture that formed them in the first place. This is a great place for your rooks to get involved from.

ISOLATED PAWN

An *isolated pawn* is a group of one. An *isolani* (another way of referring to the isolated pawn) is a pawn with no friendly neighbors. Thus it can count on no pawn support. That makes it weak.

If, however, the isolated pawn is in the center or deep in enemy territory, then it may be strong because of the disruptive influence it can have on the enemy. When a central isolated pawn springs up, it is often the focus of both players' plans.

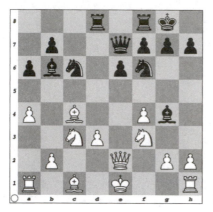

White's d3 pawn is isolated.

The side with the isolani wants to push the pawn forward, further disrupting the enemy forces, while the side fighting against it wants to stop it from moving.

A great way to fight against a central isolated pawn is to blockade it. That means to place a piece in front of it so it cannot move. The best piece for such a blockade is generally considered to be the knight.

While the isolated pawn is thus blockaded, you can build up an attack against it, forcing the opponent to use pieces as defenders. Pieces being used to defend pawns aren't doing a lot of attacking.

PASSED PAWN

A *passed pawn* is one that is free from any enemy pawn interference. As it marches up the board, the passed pawn will encounter no enemy pawns, either on its own file or on either adjacent file.

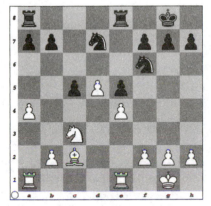

White's d5 pawn is passed.

The tremendous strength of a passed pawn is that it is a candidate to promote. The farther it has advanced up the board, the more menacing it becomes. Therefore, a passed pawn is said to have a lust to expand. Besides capturing such a pawn, the next best way of dealing with it is to blockade it, just as with an isolated pawn.

A *pawn majority* is a case of two pawns against one pawn, or three pawns against two pawns, etc., on one side of the board. The object of a pawn majority is to produce a strong passed pawn.

One way to break up such a majority is for the weaker party to attack the stronger party. This is the minority attack. The object of a minority attack is to produce a weak isolated pawn to play against.

Whenever Possible, Operate with Threats

This is so important that it gets its own chapter (see Chapter 7). There are many chess books written on this topic alone, and paying attention to threats may be the biggest difference between strong and weak players.

Very simply, if you don't notice that your queen is in danger when you make your move, you might lose her. If you don't notice that you can checkmate you opponent's king in two moves, you may not go on to win the game. If you don't notice that your king is about to come under attack, you may not be able to find a good defense.

If this sounds like you have to pay close attention to possible threats on every move of every game, that's because it is the only way to become a strong player. Sherlock Holmes, with his excellent eye for minute detail and his awareness of clues that everyone could see but few could interpret, would have made a strong chess player.

CHAPTER 6

The Importance of the Opening

The opening moves of a chess game are among the most studied parts of the contest. Masters often spend years memorizing scores of openings and their variations. *Modern Chess Openings*, a bible for any serious chess player, was first published in 1911 and is now in its fifteenth edition. It runs to 768 pages, crammed with dozens of openings and their variants. *The Oxford Companion to Chess* enumerates more than 1,300 openings.

Openings are often named for those who either invented or popularized them (Ruy Lopez Opening, Ponziani's Opening, Alekhine's Defense), and sometimes for their central move or strategy (Queen's Gambit, King's Fianchetto Opening, Bishop's Opening).

While you can find extensive discussions of openings online or invest in one of the many books that list openings, most players concentrate on learning the general principles of the opening game. In this chapter, that's pretty much what we'll do. Others seek to master two or three openings, learning the variants and the defenses against them.

Principles of the Opening

We've already talked about the importance of the central squares of the board, so it should come as no surprise to you that most openings are concerned with establishing early control of the center. In addition, openings strive to develop pieces, clear lines for those pieces to move along, and pose threats to the opponent. Of course, at the same time you must protect the king from possible threats.

Openings fall into five general categories: 1. e4 e5; 1. e4 something else; 1. d4 d5; 1. d4 something else; and 1. something else. These categories are rather wide, and there is sometimes some overlap.

HYPERMODERNISM

Classical chess theory says that the best way to control the center is to move pawns and pieces into it as soon as possible. However, in the years after the First World War an alternate school of thought emerged called hypermodernism. Its proponents argued that the center could be controlled indirectly or from a distance. The foremost exponent of this school was Grandmaster Aron Nimzowitsch (1886–1935). Among the many openings associated with this school are the Nimzo-Indian Defense, King's Indian Defense, and the Catalan Opening.

CONTROL THE CENTER

Control of the center is one clear reason why so many chess openings begin with either 1. e4 or 1. d4. The e4 move in particular simultaneously controls d5 and f5 while opening a diagonal for the king's bishop along the f1–a6 diagonal as well as for the queen along the d1–h5 diagonal. Moreover, the pawn can easily be supported by a number of moves: d3, Nc3, or f3. White has made a substantial thrust into the middle of the board and should be able to control the action of the next few moves.

However, don't get carried away by the power of your pawns in the opening. If you start to move all your pawns, you're weakening your line guarding the king. You should avoid, if at all possible, moving the pawn in front of a castled king, since this will leave the king vulnerable to attack.

WHITE'S ADVANTAGE

White holds a considerable advantage in every chess game because it moves first. This means that Black's opening move is usually a response to White, allowing White to determine the style of opening that will be played. (That isn't to say that Black is out of options; many analyses of chess openings are devoted to determining Black's best response to White's opening move.) It's been said by some analysts that White always plays to win, while Black plays not to lose.

PROTECT THE KING

As mentioned, another principal goal of the opening is to protect your king and threaten that of your opponent. Since, as we previously said, an inevitable part of the game is that your pawns move away from the king, leaving him vulnerable, you must find ways to ensure his safety.

The best way to do this is castling early. Castling gives the king strong protection, as well as helping to develop the rook, a powerful piece. The three pawns in front of the king are a powerful hedge against attacks, and for this reason you should be cautious about moving them, especially early in the game.

DEVELOPING PIECES

Developing your pieces gets them from the back row out into the midst of the board where they can start to play a role in the game. This is extremely important, since rooks and bishops can control many squares at once (ranks and files in the case of rooks, and diagonals in the case of bishops). Only the knight is capable of jumping over the pawns in front of it to enter the game in the first few moves. Therefore, another object of the opening is to allow for the development of your pieces. The more you can develop pieces and use them to control the center and expand your space, the more likely you are to win.

When developing pieces, move them to squares where they have the greatest freedom of movement and can control the largest number of squares. There's no point in getting your pieces out from behind the pawn ranks only to have them cramped and unable to do you any real good.

All this advice comes with a warning, however. Knights and bishops should be developed first, generally before the rooks. The king's rook is, in any case, often developed by castling. You should also be careful about bringing out your queen too early in the game. It's tempting to do so, because she's such a powerful piece and can put a lot of pressure on your opponent. However, a queen that is developed too early will become the target of frequent attacks, which can be distracting and use up your time.

AVOID MOVING THE SAME PIECE MULTIPLE TIMES

Openings try to accomplish their objects in as few moves as possible. This means that you should avoid moving the same piece several times whenever you can.

TEMPO

Each turn in chess is called a *tempo*. If a player moves a piece twice in a row, she's generally considered to have "lost a tempo." For instance, if White moves his knight to a certain square and Black responds by using his bishop to threaten the knight, White can reply by moving the knight to a safe square, but in so doing he's lost a tempo. Tempos are rarely decisive, but a player who consistently loses tempos is unlikely to win many games.

Two Openings

With all these points in mind, we're going to look at two openings and see how they perform the functions we've discussed.

RUY LOPEZ

As previously mentioned, this is among the oldest known and studied openings in chess. It's named for Ruy López de Segura (c. 1530–c. 1580), who discussed it in his book *Book of the Liberal Invention and Art of the Game of Chess,* published in 1561.

The opening is: **1. e4 e5 2. Nf3 Nc6 3. Bb5.**

From this point, the opening can develop in a number of directions. However, let's consider what's been accomplished so far.

The opening moves of the Ruy Lopez.

White now has a pawn in the crucial four center squares. As well, its knight threatens Black's e5 pawn and controls d4. The bishop has been developed along the f1–a6 diagonal. And the king is now in a position to castle. Black's most obvious line of defense is 3. ...a6, threatening the bishop, which retreats to a4. (This is called the Morphy Defense after Paul Morphy (1837–1884), an American grandmaster who was one of the people to develop and study it.) By the a4 move, White continues the threat to Black's knight and retains the possibility of a pin (see Chapter 7 for further discussion of pins). Black can counter with 4. ...b5, which breaks the pin and again threatens White's bishop.

This diagram shows the Open Defense, a major variant of the Ruy Lopez. Black replies with 3. ...a6 4. Ba4 Nf6 5. 0-0 Nxe4. Black is trying to assert a position in the center of the board.

In addition, over the years a number of variations have been developed on this opening in which Black responds with something other than 3. ...a6. Options include 3. ...Bc5, which develops one of Black's bishops (this variation is called the Cordel Defense); 3. ...d6, which relieves pressure on Black's e5 pawn as well as allowing the development of the queen's bishop (this is called the Old Steinitz Defense); and Bird's Defense, 3. ...Nd4, threatening White's b5 bishop as well as putting pressure on the f3 knight.

This discussion should give you an idea of how openings are discussed by chess players. Now let's look at another one.

THE QUEEN'S GAMBIT

A *gambit* is a tactic in which you offer a piece or pawn to your opponent for capture. If he accepts the gambit, he takes the piece or pawn; you take advantage of this to place yourself in a better position.

The Queen's Gambit, played since at least the fifteenth century, consists of: **1. d4 d5 2. c4.**

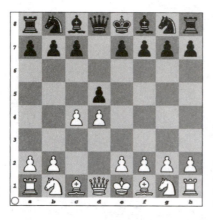

The opening moves of the Queen's Gambit. Black must now decide whether to accept or decline the gambit by capturing the c4 pawn.

White offers Black the c4 pawn to draw his opponent away from the center and leave clear lines of development for his queen's bishop and knight (the counterpart to this opening is the King's Gambit, which takes place in the e- and f-files). The two obvious lines of variation depend on whether the gambit is accepted or declined.

The classic decline of the gambit is 2. ...e6. This protects the e5 pawn while opening the f8–a3 diagonal for the king's bishop development. However, it does so at the cost of blocking the development of his other, light-colored, bishop. Thus the next section of the game will be devoted to Black's efforts to free this bishop and open the center of the board.

The Queen's Gambit Declined. Black has elected to play along one of the major variants: 3. Nc3 Nf6 4. Bg5 Be7 5. e3 0-0 6. Nf3.

The Queen's Gambit Accepted presents a different set of problems. Black takes the proffered pawn with **2. ...dxc4**. The main line of variations after this goes as follows: **3 Nf3 Nf6 4. e3 e6 5. Bxc4 c5 6. 0-0**. Play this out on a chessboard so you can see exactly what it looks like. By the end, White has completed the exchange of material; each side has now lost a pawn. Both sides have strong possibilities for development, though White is in a somewhat stronger position. Furthermore, White has castled, protecting his king. There are other variations, which you can find in books on chess openings.

Focus on Principles

If you're a beginning player who wants to improve your opening strategy, the solution is *not* to sit down and memorize a bunch of openings and all their variations. Rather, focus first on the principles of good openings. As you absorb these principles and as you study the game more, you'll find an array of openings that you like and suit your style of play. They'll become part of your chess repertoire and you can return to them again and again.

CHAPTER 7

Special Attacks

It's time to learn a bit more about what the pieces can do. Some of these special tactics can be executed by a single piece, while others can only be pulled off with a combination of pieces. The special tactics you are about to learn include the double attack, fork, discovered attack, discovered check, pin, and skewer.

Double Attack

There are special tactics that involve a *double attack*. The idea is simple: Attack one piece and your opponent will probably be able to defend it or move it easily enough. But when you attack more than one piece, your opponent has to stretch his resources, finding a way to cover everything that is under attack. That can be much more challenging than taking care of one problem at a time.

So how can you attack more than one piece at the same time? You can only move one piece at a time, after all. Actually there are various ways to do this. They are based on the principle of making full use of your pieces.

Fork

The *fork* is the easiest of the double attacks to understand. One piece attacks two or more, making use of its potential. Every piece is capable of delivering a forking attack, and even the lowly pawn can pull this one off.

In each example, you will see the position before the fork and the position after the fork. For convenience, a Black piece will do all the forking attacks in each set of positions.

Perhaps you will be surprised to know that the king can also execute a fork. But why not? The king can move in many different directions, after all. It's just necessary to slip him in between two enemies by attacking their weak spots. That is, attack them where they cannot strike back.

QUEEN FORK

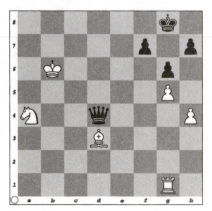

The queen threatens rook, bishop, knight, and pawn along with the check. After White gets out of check, with, say, 2. Nc5, Black will play 2. ... Qxg1.

ROOK FORK

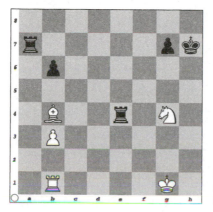

White will either lose the bishop or the knight. He cannot save both.

BISHOP FORK

The Black bishop forks the White king and queen. All White can do is get something for the queen with 2. Qxd4 Rxd4.

KNIGHT FORK

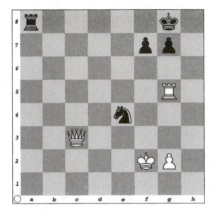

White must move the king, whereupon Black pockets the queen.

KING FORK

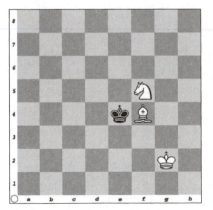

White cannot save both pieces, so must lose one and with it all checkmating opportunities.

PAWN FORK

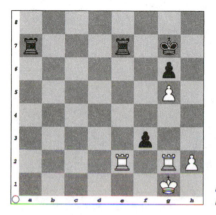

Black gets one of the White rooks.

CENTER FORK TRICK

One of the best-known combinations in the early part of the game is the center fork trick. In it, Black temporarily gives up a piece in order to regain it later with additional central control and open lines to bring out the rest of his pieces: **1. e4 e5 2. Nf3 Nc6 3. Bc4 Nf6 4. Nc3.**

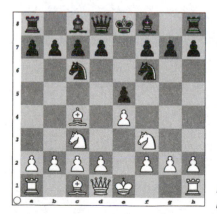

Here is where Black gives up the piece: 4. ... Nxe4 5. Nxe4.

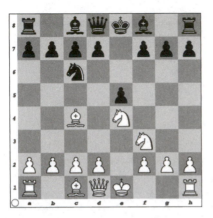

And here is where he regains it with the center fork trick: 5. ... d5.

Discovered Attack

This one is more complicated. A *discovered attack* requires a player to use two friendly pieces on the same move. The way to do that is to make use of the long-range power of queen, rook, or bishop. The long-range piece is masked by almost anything at all—king, pawn, knight, rook, or bishop—and the masking piece moves out of the way.

PRECONDITIONS FOR A DISCOVERED ATTACK

As long as there is an enemy piece or pawn on the line that contains the long-range piece and the masking piece, we have a discovered attack.

THE ATTACKING PIECE

This is the essence of a long-range piece's attacking power. The piece sits in an unobtrusive, out-of-the-way place, and radiates power outward. In order for a discovered attack to function, one of these pieces has to be lined up with another friendly piece in front of it, and an enemy piece further along the same rank or file.

Here is a discovered attack about to happen, using the knight and queen:

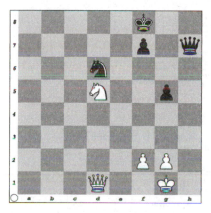

White plays 1. Nf6 attacking knight and queen.

THE MASKING PIECE

This can be any piece except a queen—even a king or a pawn. As long as it has the power to get out of the way, you've got the ingredients for a discovered attack.

Here are two more examples where a king and pawn are used as the masking piece that gets out of the way. It is White to move in this example.

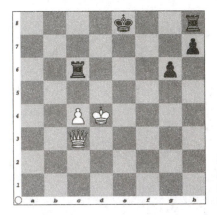

White plays 1. Kd5 and both rooks are en prise (meaning they are undefended and under attack).

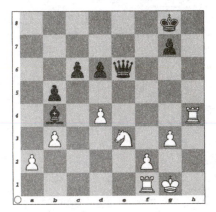

After 1. d5, White is attacking the queen, c6 pawn, and bishop for a triple attack.

THE ENEMY PIECE

There is no discovered attack if there is nothing to attack. So the third ingredient for a successful discovered attack is the enemy piece. Of course, the more powerful or important the enemy piece, the better. In the examples, we saw enemy queens, rooks, bishops, knights, and even a pawn attacked by way of a discovered attack.

This last ingredient is really what makes discovered attacks so strong and hard to defend. In each of the cases we looked at, the discovered attack was particularly effective because both White pieces were threatening to capture something.

MORE EFFECTIVE DISCOVERED ATTACKS

It is possible to play a discovered attack where the long-range piece being uncovered is the only one attacking anything. But it's generally much more effective if the unmasking piece can also attack something.

The idea behind the discovered attack is just plain good chess. It pays to know it well. Here is a trap that shows how important such knowledge is:

1. d4 d5 2. c4 e6 3. Nc3 c6 4. Nf3 f5 5. Qc2 Nf6 6. Bg5 Bd6 7. Bxf6 Qxf6 8. cxd5 cxd5.

Play it out on a board to see how it looks.

DISCOVERED DEFENSE

This idea is less well known, but still important. It can be used to defend all sorts of things while continuing with a plan of development and center control when something is being attacked. Here is an example of discovered defense in action:

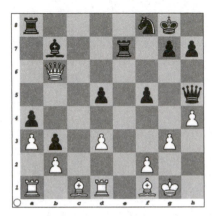

White to move doesn't want to move the en prise d1 rook since there's nowhere good to put it. But he can let the a1 rook do the defending and even threaten something himself with 1. Bg5.

Discovered Check

This is nothing more than a special form of discovered attack. The reason this move is special lies in the piece under attack. It happens to be the enemy king; thus it results in a check. Since checks are so important, this is one of your most effective tools in a chess game. The check comes from seemingly nowhere, since the piece you move does not do the checking.

EXAMPLES OF DISCOVERED CHECK

Here is a wonderful example of a discovered check.

1. e4 e5 2. Nf3 Nf6 3. Nxe5 d6 4. Nf3 Nxe4 5. d4 Bg4 6. h3 Bh5 7. Qd3 Qe7.

Alarm bells should go off in White's head. The Black queen is on the same file as his king! But White sees a fork that comes with a check, and so lacks a proper sense of danger.

8. Qb5+.

Here it is: a three-pronged fork on the Black king, b7 pawn, and h5 bishop.

8. ... c6.

This little pawn move threatens the queen, gets out of check, and defends the b7 pawn with a discovered defense. Of course, the bishop on h5 is still en prise. But it's nothing more than juicy bait.

9. Qxh5.

There is a surprise in store for White, whose king and enemy queen are on the same e-file, along with an enemy knight.

9. ... Nf6+.

This discovered check takes White by complete surprise. The knight does the moving, threatening the White queen along the way. But it is the Black queen that does the checking.

You may be wondering if the shielding piece can deliver a check. Of course! Any piece or pawn can deliver a check at any time during a game, provided the enemy king is within range. Discovered check refers to a situation where the long-range piece is "discovered" giving check after the shielding piece moves out of the way. But the shielding piece can deliver check in an otherwise normal discovered attack. Here is an example with White to move:

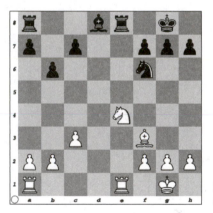

White wins the exchange with the discovered attack 1. Nxf6+.

The discovered attack is on the rook, and the shielding piece is giving check.

1. ... Bxf6 2. Bxa8 Rxa8.

DOUBLE CHECK

Since either piece can deliver check in a double attack, one wonders whether both can do so at the same time. And in fact they can. This little bit of overkill is known as a *double check*.

When both pieces deliver check at the same time, the enemy is placed in an immediate quandary. Just think back to the three possible ways out of check. In a double check you cannot block the check, since you will only be blocking one of the two checks. You also can't capture the checking piece unless you do so with the king itself, since otherwise the other checking piece would still be checking. The only way to defend against a double check is to move the king! Thus a double check often has devastating power.

Here are some examples of that most powerful weapon, the double check.

1. d4 d5 2. c4 c6 3. Nc3 Nf6 4. Nf3 Bg4 5. Ne5 Bf5 6. g3 Nbd7 7. Bg2 e6 8. 0–0 Nxe5 9. dxe5 Nd7 10. cxd5 exd5 11. e4 dxe4 12. g4 Bg6 13. Nxe4 Nxe5 14. Bf4 Nd3 15. Qe2.

White sets up a double check that is most efficient.

If Black takes the bait with 15. ... Nxf4, we get 16. Nf6#. This is a checkmate even though both checking pieces are en prise. Remarkable! Furthermore, if Black wants to wait a move to take the bait, we get 15. ... Bxe4 16. Bxe4 Nxf4 17. Bxc6#.

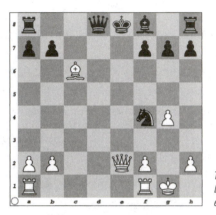

This is another checkmate while both checking pieces remain en prise.

Pin

This is a weapon that requires two enemy pieces on the same line with a friendly long-range piece. Instead of two good guys and one bad guy on the line, as in a discovered attack, we have one good guy holding two bad guys hostage. Well, only one of them is actually held hostage, but they both have to be there.

The *pin* is more akin to a wrestling pin than to a sewing pin. In it, one friendly long-range piece looks at a powerful enemy piece with a less powerful enemy piece shielding it.

Here's an example of a pin early in the game.

1. e4 e5 2. Nf3 d6 3. d4 Bg4.

The White knight is pinned to the queen.

4. dxe5 Bxf3 5. Qxf3.

This eliminates the pin. But we're not yet done.

5. ... dxe5 6. Bc4 Nf6 7. Qb3 Qe7 8. Nc3 c6 9. Bg5.

White has countered by pinning the Black knight to the queen, a pin that will stay around for a while.

9. ... b5 10. Nxb5 cxb5 11. Bxb5+ Nbd7.

We swing into the last part of the game with the Black knight pinned to the king.

12. 0-0-0 Rd8 13. Rxd7 Rxd7.

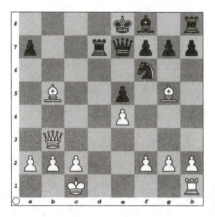

*Now it is the rook that is pinned
to the king.*

14. Rd1 Qe6 15. Bxd7+ Nxd7 16. Qb8+ Nxb8 17. Rd8#.

ABSOLUTE PIN

On move 11 of the game you just looked at, Black moves a knight in the way of the checking bishop and the king. This blocks the check, so is good. But it also puts Black into an *absolute pin*— that is, a pin in which the pinned piece (the knight on d7) not only shouldn't move, but can't move.

Whenever a piece lies between your king and an enemy long-range piece, it is in an absolute pin. It cannot move out of the line of fire, since you are not allowed to place your king in check.

PIN AND REPIN

One of the best ways to take advantage of a pinned piece is to hit it again and again. If you want to break down your opponent's defenses, harsh measures are called for. So when you spy an immobile piece, such as a pinned piece, attack it again. This is much more effective than simply exchanging the pinning piece for the pinned piece.

Skewer

A *skewer*, sometimes referred to as an *x-ray attack*, is sort of a mirror-image pin. It requires a long-range piece and two enemy pieces on the same line of attack, just like a pin does, but in a skewer the more important or powerful piece is doing the shielding. Therefore, instead of immobilizing the piece, a skewer practically forces it to move, thus exposing the poor little guy it had shielded. When the two enemy pieces are of the same value, it is referred to as a *skewer*, rather than a pin.

Here is an example of a skewer in action.

This position, with Black to move, came up at a regional tournament in the Midwest during the mid-1990s.

DOUBLE ATTACKS

Pins and skewers are nothing more than specialized forms of double attack. It's just that both enemy pieces stand on the same line, so the attacking is being done through one piece on the other.

The player handling the Black pieces didn't notice a short combination leading to a skewer, and so failed to defeat the chess master he was playing.

First, notice that White threatens to win a rook, since he has a battery of rooks on the d-file. Black can move his rook out of the way with 1. ... Rdc8, or by exchanging rooks. Here's what happens if he exchanges rooks:

1. ... Rxd2 2. Rxd2.

Set the position up on a board and play it out. Do you see the skewer now? Simply look for any two White pieces on the same line as one of your long-range pieces (you've only got two), and you will see it.

2. ... Bc1!

Here it is. The rook is more powerful than the knight. If it moves out of the way, Black will simply capture the knight:

3. Rd7 Bxg5.

The best defense is to let the rook go with 3. Nf3. That way, White at least gets the bishop for the rook after 3. ... Bxd2 4. Nxd2.

More Attacks

There are many kinds of tactical setups that require more than two pieces. These include convergence and batteries (two friendly pieces going after an enemy) and discovered attacks of various sorts (two friendly pieces going after more than one enemy). Some of these we've discussed in this chapter: forks (one piece going after more than one enemy) and pins and skewers (one piece going after two enemies). These are part of your arsenal of weapons in chess.

CHAPTER 8

The Next Few Moves

Throughout most of a game, you cannot reasonably plan a checkmate. So what is left to plan? A lot. You can plan to specifically improve your position within the next couple of moves, or you can come up with a general theme you want to promote. The former is referred to as *tactics*, and the latter is referred to as *strategy*.

Tactics

These short-term plans can encompass anything that will help you to improve your position or interfere with your opponent's position. When you bring a new piece into play—controlling a center square and preparing to castle, for instance—that is part of your tactical plan. (Castling itself can often fit in well with such short-term goals. It helps to bring your rook to the middle while helping to hide your king away behind a wall of pawns.)

STRATEGY VERSUS TACTICS

Long-range, general goals for the future are *strategic plans*. They include gaining control of key squares, creating and pushing a passed pawn, using all your pieces, and exposing your opponent's king. More immediate goals of improving your position and/or destroying your opponent's position are *tactics*. These include various forms of double attack and any immediate threats.

BUILDING FOR THE FUTURE

Short-term plans are considered tactical because they offer immediate improvement of your position. You also need to think long-term in determining where to place your pieces, though, since you want them to be available later in the game. So placing a piece in the center where it will immediately perish is generally not a good idea.

You have to see far enough ahead on each move to know whether your move is safe. Am I placing this piece en prise? Will my opponent be able to attack this piece in the next couple of moves? Am I leaving anything open to attack by moving this piece? These are the kinds of questions you must answer before deciding on a particular move.

THREATS

The general idea of what tactics is all about centers on immediate, violent threats. You threaten a checkmate or to capture a piece, and your opponent responds with a threat to capture one of your pieces or checkmate your king. These threats can take many forms, and you learn more about them in Chapter 9.

This violence—the threat to capture pieces, often combined with actual captures—is the most appealing and also the most difficult part of tactics. You absolutely have to be aware of all threats as well as all their consequences in order to be able to play a strong game.

WHAT'S A COMBINATION?

A *combination* is a planned series of tactical moves using captures, checks, and threats of all sorts to gain an advantage or wipe out a disadvantage. Most combinations involve at least a temporary sacrifice of some sort, giving up something of importance in order to reap the rewards a little later.

Planning a tactical sequence involves seeing ahead several moves. But more importantly, it involves judging the consequences of the sequence. For instance, consider the following position:

With Black to move, the first thing that should spring to mind is that White threatens to invade on f7, capturing a pawn with either bishop or knight.

You can try various defenses, such as 1. ... Nh6, 1. ... Be6, 1. ... Qe7, or 1. ... Bxe5. Look at them all and assess the consequences.

1. Nh6 brings a new piece into play, but doesn't attempt to control central squares. Further, are you ready to meet 2. Bxh6 in a way that both recaptures the piece and saves the f7 pawn?

1. ... Be6 goes for the center and even threatens to capture the White bishop. But are you ready to answer 2. Bxe6 with 2. ... fxe6, exposing your king and ruining your pawns?

1. ... Qe7 doesn't really defend the pawn at all. White plays 2. Nxf7, picking off the pawn clean, and even getting the rook in the corner.

But 1. ... Bxe5 saves the pawn while getting rid of that annoying knight. White can threaten the pawn again, along with checkmate, by playing 2. Qh5, but 2. ... Qe7 seems to defend everything adequately while bringing another piece into play.

Strategy

Long-range plans may involve some immediate threats as an incidental part of the strategy, but mostly we are looking at a general build-up over many moves. These long-range plans can also be looked at as threats, but they lack the immediacy of tactical threats, so strategic threats are subtler.

TYPES OF PLANS

Of course the ultimate idea behind all plans is to eventually get a checkmate, or at least to avoid getting checkmated. But a plan to checkmate can only be successful if there is some way to get at the opposing king. Against an experienced opponent, that sort of situation isn't easy to set up. So during most of the game, you will be working with more modest goals.

A typical early strategic plan is to bring out all your pieces in order to control the center. Once you have accomplished that, the next stage might be to force a breach in your opponent's pawns or to get a bishop pair on an open board working against two knights or a bishop and a knight. Or, you might work to create a passed pawn or to get a powerful knight posted in your opponent's territory. Another strategic goal could be to double up your rooks on a file in order to penetrate to your opponent's half of the board. Or it could be simply to expose the enemy king to an attack.

BOOK UP!

There are literally hundreds of books on chess strategy and planning that are available in your local library, through the USCF (United States Chess Federation), or on the Internet. Chess magazines of all types usually have a section or several articles devoted to this very important aspect of the game. Even computers are getting into the act, with software available that teaches how to form and carry out a game plan.

CARRYING OUT THE PLAN

Once you get the hang of forming strategic plans, your only trouble will be carrying them out. After all, your opponent will be trying to stop you. It's something like deciding to walk to the corner store in an unfriendly neighborhood or in the middle of a blizzard. You can do it, but it requires courage, persistence, and preparation.

Your strategic plans have to be realistic, or you'll never be able to carry them out. At the same time, plans that are too modest won't get you very far either, even if you do carry them out. For instance, if you plan to draw your game, the trouble is that you just might succeed. In such a case, you never had a chance to win because you never tried.

Seeing Ahead

All plans, whether short-term or long-term, require that you see into the future at least a bit. You have to be able to predict what the chances of success will be with any given plan. With a combination, as long as it isn't too complex, you can often see right through to the end of the captures and threats. Then it's a matter of counting up what is left and assessing the results. A strategic plan is often harder to see through to conclusion before you begin, because there are so many things that can go wrong when you don't account for specifics.

STRIKE IF YOU HAVE THE ADVANTAGE

When you have the advantage, you must attack, or you will lose your advantage. But beware of two things: First, make sure you really have a big advantage. Second, make sure you can find a way to continue the attack. Otherwise, your advantage can disappear through timidity or poor tactics.

A great way to carry out a strategic theme is to use threats and combinations to back up your theme. The following game fragment is a case in point:

1. d4 d5 2. c4 dxc4 3. Nf3 c5 4. e3 a6 5. Bxc4 b5.

Position after 5. ... b5.

White has completed the first part of his plan from the beginning. He has developed bishop and knight aggressively and controls the center. Meanwhile, Black has only moved pawns. Not a single Black piece is moved yet.

But White is confronted with a dilemma. His bishop is under attack. What to do? It feels wrong to retreat the bishop when White has the only pieces in play and controls the center. The strategic plan demands an attack.

So common sense and tactics come to the aid of strategy. White controls the a2–g8 diagonal. Black's king is the only defender of his f7 pawn, which is on that diagonal. The a8–h1 diagonal also beckons, since Black has an undefended rook sitting there at a8, and White has a queen ready to go to f3. There is a very nice, strong, central outpost for White's knight on e5.

Can we make use of all these features of the position? Yes, we can, with the following combination: **6. Bxf7+.** White sacrifices bishop for pawn with the idea of bringing the Black king out into the open, vulnerable to a White knight on e5 and a White queen on f3.

6. ... Kxf7 7. Ne5+ Ke8 8. Qf3.

White threatens checkmate on f7 and the en prise a8 rook. One of them will have to go.

8. ... Nf6 9. Qxa8.

And White has won the Exchange for a pawn, and exposed the Black king as well.

Another way to carry out the same idea is with a different move order: **6. Ne5**. White threatens 7. Bxf7#.

6. ... bxc4 7. Qf3.

Now White threatens 8. Qxf7# as well as the en prise rook.

7. ... Nf6 8. Qxa8.

And White has won the Exchange.

WHAT IF MY OPPONENT DOESN'T GO ALONG WITH MY PLAN?

If your plan is good, this shouldn't matter. A good plan takes all reasonable moves and plans into account. If your opponent tries something unreasonable, chances are it will be bad, and he just did you a favor. But if his move is both good and unexpected, you should take time to reassess the situation. You might also have resources that you didn't foresee.

Planning Greater Force

A frequent strategic plan is to win material. This comes in different forms, ranging from winning a free pawn to winning the Exchange to promoting a pawn and thus suddenly going up a whole queen.

This kind of plan will only work under the right conditions, however. And such plans often run the risk of allowing your opponent a different kind of advantage, such as giving her more squares or a good attacking position.

CONDITIONS FOR WINNING MATERIAL

In order to have a reasonable amount of success with a plan of winning material, you have to have some idea of what material you are going to win. And that material must be weakened in some way. The material you're after should meet one or more of the following conditions. It should be:

- Underdefended
- Undefended
- Exposed
- Too far away
- Unable to move

Under those conditions, you should have a reasonable chance of winning the desired material.

In the last example, the a8 rook was undefended and exposed, so it should not be surprising that White was able to plan for its capture.

WHAT ARE YOU GIVING UP?

This one is harder to judge. Again in the last example, Black tried to win the White bishop. The problem with his plan was that it succeeded! His win of the bishop ultimately cost him his king's safety, the center, and his poor, exposed rook.

There are pieces and pawns left unattended every day that are best left alone. One example should suffice:

1. d4 Nf6 2. c4 e5 3. dxe5 Ng4 4. Bf4 Nc6 5. Nf3 Bb4+ 6. Nbd2 Qe7.

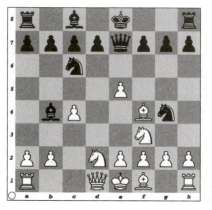

Position after 6. ... Qe7.

Black has been bringing out new pieces with every turn, focusing on the e5 pawn, and is now poised to win it. This will recover the pawn he sacrificed back on move 2. White decides to mess up the Black plan by threatening to capture the bishop on b4, which certainly seems like a reasonable thing to do.

7. a3 Ncxe5.

But Black leaves the bishop en prise and recovers his pawn instead. Does this make sense? He could have played 7. ... Bxd2+ easily enough, after all.

8. axb4.

White believes that Black simply overlooked that the bishop was en prise. But it was White who overlooked something important. What did White fail to note?

8. ... Nd3#.

He was not aware that his king had no possible moves, or perhaps he was unacquainted with this particular checkmate. What a harsh way to find out!

Traps introduced by seemingly absurd giveaways lurk everywhere in the game of chess. Yet you can't simply avoid capturing anything that is offered. Such an attitude is far too timid, and won't help win games. The best way to solve this dilemma is to look all gift horses in the mouth before deciding whether or not to make the capture. Analyze the consequences of each and every capture, and you will go a long way toward playing a strong chess game.

Controlling the Center

Both players strive for this from the very beginning; at least, they do if they are experienced players. So how can you wrest the center away from someone who is trying as hard as you are for its control?

The simple answer is to focus all your resources on controlling those essential squares. While planning to win material, while planning an attack on the king, while planning to bring all your pieces into the game, and while keeping a sharp eye out for tactical opportunities, don't forget to focus all your moves on the center.

There is more than one way to go about controlling the center. In fact, there are essentially two ways: You can strive for the classical pawn center, or you can try for the hypermodern center.

THE CLASSICAL PAWN CENTER

This approach boils down to "put your pawns in the center and keep them there." At the end of the nineteenth century, the chess giant and first world champion Wilhelm Steinitz promoted this kind of center, and at the turn of the twentieth century, the famous chess teacher and author Siegbert Tarrasch codified the idea. Tarrasch went so far as to suggest that without a strong pawn center your game would likely collapse.

The idea is simple enough. Since pawns are the least powerful members of the chess family, place them side by side in the center and you deny any central squares to your opponent's pieces.

A great example of fighting for central control with pawns is the following opening variation:

1. e4 c6 2. d3 d5 3. Nd2 e5 4. Ngf3.

Black has more pawns in the center than White does, but White has more pieces in play. White also threatens to win the e5 pawn.

4. ... Nd7 5. d4.

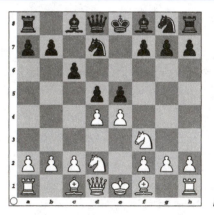

Position after 5. d4.

White once again threatens to win the e5 pawn, and still has more pieces in play. And notice that both sides have filled up the entire center with pawns.

THE HYPERMODERN CENTER

This is an idea that has always been known, but wasn't often used early in the game. It is really a counterattacking idea. The so-called *hypermoderns* decided that a big, fat pawn center can make a great target for an attack by the pieces. So they came up with ways to avoid putting pawns in the center. Instead, they set up positions to attack their opponent's pawns, which were always obligingly there in the center.

Getting All Your Pieces Involved

This is another plan that every good player uses. It is sometimes not easy to understand how you can get all the pieces into the game when you can only move one with each move. But patience, good judgment, and a sharp eye for tactics will make this plan readily available.

AN EXAMPLE

The following game, which you've already seen (in Chapter 7), is a model of developing every piece purposefully. Watch how White brings new pieces into play using threats at nearly every turn. Those few moves when a new piece is not brought into play involve capturing and threatening to capture. (White: Paul Morphy; Black: Duke and Count; Paris, 1857.)

1. e4 e5 2. Nf3.

A new piece comes to the center, threatening the e5 pawn.

2. ... d6 3. d4.

Lines are opened for the queen and the c1 bishop, while there is a threat to the e5 pawn.

3. ... Bg4 4. dxe5.

This move opens up the d-file for the queen and grabs a pawn.

4. ... Bxf3 5. Qxf3.

This recovers the piece, saves the queen, and gets the queen into the action.

5. ... dxe5 6. Bc4.

A new piece comes into play with a checkmate threat on f7. Kingside castling is also prepared.

6. ... Nf6 7. Qb3.

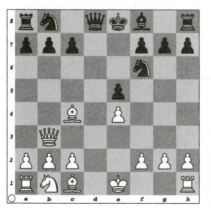

This transfer of an already developed piece comes with two threats: one to the underdefended f7 pawn, and the other to the undefended b7 pawn.

7. ... Qe7 8. Nc3.

A new piece comes in play, defending the e4 pawn.

8. ... c6 9. Bg5.

A new piece comes in play, preparing queenside castling.

9. ... b5 10. Nxb5.

The bishop is saved at the cost of the knight. White will get two pawns for the knight along with an enduring attack on the uncastled Black king.

10. ... cxb5 11. Bxb5+.

The bishop comes into even more powerful play, checking and getting the second pawn.

11. ... Nbd7 12. 0–0–0.

The king gets tucked safely away while the rook commands the d-file.

12. ... Rd8 13. Rxd7.

This move serves to expose the enemy king while making room on d1 for the other rook.

13. ... Rxd7 14. Rd1.

White gets the last piece in play, threatening a destructive exchange on d7.

14. ... Qe6 15. Bxd7+. This move captures the rook and checks the king while making extra room on the b-file for the queen.

15. ... Nxd7 16. Qb8+. This check gives up the queen but forces Black to open the d-file for the White rook.

16. ... Nxb8 17. Rd8#.

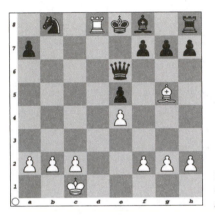

With this checkmate, White has used every piece to its maximum potential.

DEVELOP NEW PIECES

Developing a new piece with each turn, as far as possible, is essential to good chess play. Here is an example of what happens when one player heeds this advice and the other player doesn't:

1. e4 c5 2. d4 cxd4 3. c3 dxc3.

White is playing a gambit, in which he gives up a pawn in order to bring more pieces into the center quickly.

4. Nxc3 Nc6 5. Bc4 Nf6 6. Nf3 d6.

White's queen and bishop command nice open lines, while he also has more pieces in play.

7. e5! Nxe5.

Black avoids the horrors of 7. ... dxe5 8. Qxd8+ Nxd8 9. Nb5 Rb8 10. Nxe5, but what he gets is worse.

8. Nxe5 dxe5 9. Bxf7+ Kxf7 10. Qxd8.

Exposing the King

This is always a good plan to have, provided you have a means of carrying it out. An exposed king can easily get checkmated, while one well shielded is harder to get at.

Consider this famous example. (Edward Lasker–Sir George Thomas. London Chess Club, 1912.)

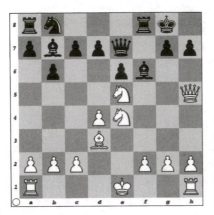

White to play. Notice before we begin the final assault that White controls the center and has four pieces in play pointed at the Black king. Winning combinations do not spring out of random positions.

11. Qxh7+!! Kxh7. The king comes out into the open. Of course, he has no choice in the matter.

12. Nxf6+ Kh6 or 12. ... Kh8 13. Ng6#. White continues to play forcing moves, keeping the Black king in check. While flying from each check, Black never has time to protect his king or win the game with his extra queen.

13. Neg4+ Kg5 14. h4+ Kf4 15. g3+ Kf3 16. Be2+ Kg2 17. Rh2+ Kg1 18. Kd2#!

The Black king has taken a strange journey to meet his demise.

SACRIFICE COMBINATIONS

The chess world is filled with combinations in which one player sacrifices his pieces in order to bring the opponent's king out into the open, where he will be vulnerable to an early checkmate. Those that work are often very beautiful and make the archives. Those that fall short serve as warnings that such attacks need to be accurately calculated.

Planning Defense

Defense is often harder to plan than an attack because it requires you to identify a potential attack to defend against. And nobody wants to contemplate the various ways in which an opponent can destroy your position.

Nevertheless, it pays off to sniff out potential attacks on your position. If you make ready for the enemy attack, it probably won't overwhelm you. So here are three good defensive plans you can use when weathering a storm.

- ▪ Trade pieces.
- ▪ Bring up extra defenders.
- ▪ Have a good attack.

TRADE PIECES

When there are too many enemy pieces swarming about your king, get rid of some of them. Trading your opponent's attacking pieces is one of the best ways to stop her attack. Here is an example:

1. e4 e5 2. Nf3 Nc6 3. d4 exd4 4. Bc4. White has given up a pawn to get more pieces in play.

4. ... Bc5 5. Ng5. White now attacks the f7 square, but fails to get a new piece in play.

5. ... Nh6 6. Qh5 Qe7.

White now recovers his pawn, but he has to trade two pieces in order to do it, and that breaks the attack.

7. Bxf7+ Nxf7 8. Nxf7 Qxf7 9. Qxc5 d6.

White has no attack. In fact, Black is attacking the lone White piece that's in play and is getting ready to bring still more pieces in play himself.

The greatest defenders can also wield powerful attacks. How could it be otherwise? In order to be able to put up a good defense, you have to be able to see the opponent's attack coming many moves in advance, perhaps even before your opponent spies it! And if you can see attacks developing that far in advance, you will certainly be able to produce a few good attacks yourself.

BRING UP EXTRA DEFENDERS

This is often a good way to put down a building attack. It stands to reason: You don't try to make a basket in basketball with a two-on-five break. That's backward. So if you surround your king with many defenders, he will be very difficult to get at.

Here is an example:

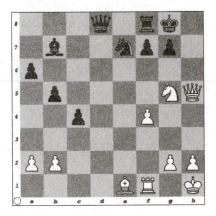

Black to move. White threatens checkmate on h7.

Black needs extra defenders, so he looks at 1. ... Be4. Since this loses the bishop, he has to try something else. Then he finds **1. ... Qd3!**, which adds an extra defender to h7 while threatening checkmate on f1.

2. Kg1 Qg6.

Black is ready to trade White's attacking queen for his own defender.

HAVE A GOOD ATTACK

The old sports saying, "The best defense is a good offense," often applies in chess as well. Take a look at the following famous combination played by Adolf Anderssen against Lionel Kieseritzky in 1851 (ever since dubbed "The Immortal Game").

White to move. White controls the center and has more pieces in play—by a lot! So instead of defending the en prise rook, he builds up the attack.

18. Bd6! Qxa1+ 19. Ke2 Bxg1.

Now White is out of rooks but still has four pieces on the attack, while Black hasn't brought out any more pieces or provided more defenders to his king.

20. e5 Na6 21. Nxg7+ Kd8.

White now forces checkmate in two moves.

22. Qf6+! Nxf6 23. Be7#.

When defending by attacking, it is essential that you make sure what you are going after is worth what you are giving up. It does no good to defend an attack on your queen by attacking an enemy rook, unless there is more to your attack. Checkmating attacks, threats to promote a pawn or two, and massive build-up of your attacking force are often worth a lot. When it comes to defending against an attack on one piece by attacking another, usually the deciding factor is what other aspects of the positions change, such as the control of the center or who has more pieces in play.

CHAPTER 9

Build Your Arsenal of Chess Tactics

Besides the various sorts of double attack, there are other tactical things the pieces can do. These include, but are not limited to, removing the defender, overload, interference, zwischenzug, desperado, and no retreat. These ideas can take place using various units of attack and defense. All are based on very sensible attacking ideas that every chess player should know.

Removing the Defender

The idea behind *removing the defender* is simply to get rid of the support a piece has. You remember that one of the ways to meet a threat to capture is to defend the threatened piece. Well, this tactic gets rid of that defender.

1. e4 e5 2. Nf3 Nc6 3. Bb5 Nf6 4. d3 a6.

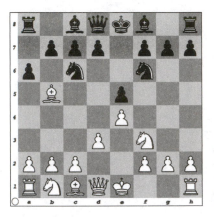

The e5 pawn is under attack by the knight on f3. It is also defended by the knight on c6. So White removes the defender and picks up the pawn for free one move later.

5. Bxc6 dxc6 6. Nxe5.

The hard part is that you have an opponent who doesn't want you to pull off any of those tricks. So you need to learn to look at whatever position is in front of you with a keen eye for any of the patterns you have learned. When one begins to take shape, play for it. The rewards will come soon enough.

Overload

A concept related to removing the defender is the overloaded piece. In this one, a piece is doing more than its fair share, and an astute opponent notices this *overload* and takes advantage of it.

1. e4 c5 2. Nf3 d6 3. g3 Nc6 4. Bg2 Bg4 5. 0–0 Nd4 6. h3.

The g2 bishop is doing double duty. It is defending both the pinned knight on f3 and the pawn on h3. Black makes use of this situation to win a pawn.

6. ...Nxf3+ 7. Bxf3 Bxh3.

Interference

Another type of overloading is shown through the subtle idea of *interference*. In this one, a piece gets in the way or interferes with two cooperating pieces. It is White to move.

First the king is driven back so he can interfere with the Black rooks defending each other:

1. Rh7+ Ke8.

Next the White queen swoops in to get at everybody:

2. Qe6+ Kd8 3. Qd6+.

We have a tragicomic situation. The rooks can defend each other as long as the Black king doesn't interfere. But there's no way for him to slip out, and one of the rooks will exit as a result of the queen's triple fork:

4. ... Kc8 5. Qxf8+.

White has picked up one of the rooks.

Zwischenzug

This one isn't as difficult as it may look or sound (the Zs are pro-nounced "ts"). *Zwischenzug* is a German word meaning "in-between move." It refers to a situation where one player responds to a threat by ignoring it temporarily in order to threaten something else that is more important. After the more important threat is seen to, the player may come back and take care of the original threat.

More often than not, a zwischenzug is a check or an attack on the queen. These are threats not easily ignored. Here is an example that happens very early:

1. e4 e5 2. Nf3 Nc6 3. d4 exd4 4. Nxd4 Bc5 5. Nxc6.

Black does not have to recapture the knight right away. Instead, he can play the zwischenzug 5. ... Qf6, which threatens checkmate.

Only after White has seen to the checkmate threat with, say, 6. Qe2 will Black recapture the knight.

The following opening trap is very interesting because it contains several zwischenzugs:

1. e4 e5 2. d4 exd4 3. Qxd4 Nf6 4. Bg5 Be7 5. e5.

And here comes the zwischenzug:

5. ... Nc6!

Black expects White to move his attacked queen. But moving the queen causes trouble. For instance, 6. Qc3 loses to the pin 6. ... Bb4, while 6. Qe3 runs into the fork and discovered attack 6. ... Ng4. So, rather than defending the queen, White plays his own zwischenzug:

6. exf6! Nxd4 7. fxe7.

And White gets the queen back after all. But just who profited the most from this series is not quite clear.

IF YOU'RE UNDER FIRE, ATTACK

A zwischenzug is simply carrying out the old sports adage "the best defense is a good offense." Always remember to take a further look at whatever threats are looming after a zwischenzug, or, as in the previous example, a series of zwischenzugs. Just make sure you always are aware of each and every threat to check or capture at all times during a game.

Desperado

The *desperado* tactic is named after the bad guys in old Westerns. If you're about to lose a piece no matter what you do, take something out with it. When you think about it, this is nothing more than plain common sense.

1. e4 e5 2. f4 Bc5 3. Nf3 Nc6 4. Bc4 d6 5. c3 Bg4.

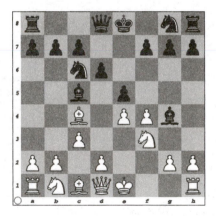

Black spies a chance to win a pawn using a discovered attack. But has she looked far enough ahead?

6. Bxf7+ Kxf7 7. Ng5+.

Here is the discovered attack. The pin is broken and the Black king is in check. Therefore, White will get back her bishop. Except for the desperado.

7. ... Qxg5!

Black sees that moving the king will result in losing the bishop. If the bishop is going to be lost, why not take something out with it? Like a knight? If the queens get exchanged after 8. fxg5 Bxd1 9. Kxd1, Black winds up with an extra piece. The same thing happens if White tries a zwischenzug with **8. Qb3+ Be6**.

If White tries her own desperado with 9. Qxe6+ Kxe6 10. fxg5, Black always winds up with an extra piece.

The reason is, he started the combination up a piece to begin with, and captured a second piece right at the start. All White could do was recover one of her pieces here with **9. Qxb7 Qd8 10. Qxc6 Qe8.**

No Retreat

When a piece has nowhere to move, simply threaten to capture it. This tactic often causes a desperado. So make sure when you trap a piece that can't move safely, that it *really* can't move safely!

A famous opening trap involves forcing a bishop into a situation in which it has no retreat. It goes like this (play this out on a board):

1. e4 e5 2. Nf3 Nc6 3. Bb5 a6 4. Ba4 Nf6 5. 0–0 Be7 6. Re1 b5 7. Bb3 d6 8. d4 exd4 9. Nxd4 Nxd4 10. Qxd4 c5 11. Qc3 c4.

As you can see, the White bishop has nowhere safe to move. The desperado **12. Bxc4 bxc4 13. Qxc4** doesn't give White enough for the piece.

This trap is so old it's affectionately referred to as the Noah's Ark trap. So if you fall for it, you're in good company.

No Retreat means no forward moves as well. When the situation comes up, the piece in question simply has nowhere safe to move.

CHAPTER 10

Dominating the Endgame

After the cut and parry of the middle game, as you bring your range of attacks and tactics to bear on your opponent, you may begin to relax as the board gradually clears of pieces and you can see lines and positions more clearly.

But rest assured, the endgame in chess can be just as complex and demanding as the opening or the middle game. Even when it comes down to only a few pieces, there are important things to watch for:

- Can your opponent find a way to promote a pawn (see Chapter 3)?
- Can she force you into stalemate, denying you a win?
- Are any of your pieces in danger?
- Is your king in danger?

One feature that distinguishes endgames is that many of the pieces, including quite likely the queens, have been removed from the board. This means that the pieces that remain have greater freedom of movement and the king becomes a more active participant in the game.

Here are some general principles to guide you in your mastery of the endgame.

Learn the Basic Checkmates

In Chapter 2 we talked about some of the basic moves to checkmate your opponent. You need to become so familiar with these patterns that you can recognize them no matter how cluttered the board is with pieces.

ZUGZWANG?

The German word *zugzwang*, which first popped up in chess literature in the middle of the nineteenth century, refers to a situation in which one player would prefer not to move because any move he makes worsens his situation. This problem tends to crop up most often in the endgame.

To this extent, you can say that *the better you play the middle game, the better you'll be at the endgame.* That isn't to say that you can relax and not think as hard when you get to the endgame, but a careful study of tactics and strategy will serve you well in the last stage of the game.

Simplify! Simplify!

If you're a piece or more ahead of your opponent, your immediate objective should be to clear the board. Exchange as much material as possible in order to get the dynamics of the play down to their purest, simplest form. Once you start to clear away material, more opportunities will start to present themselves to you for traps, pins, and so on. Sometimes you can begin this process in the middle game.

Don't get careless at this stage. Your opponent is still in the game, and a foolish move on your part can lose your advantage.

Planning Checkmate

Checkmates don't just happen randomly. You have to set them up by visualizing them in advance. Then you have to find a way to get your opponent to cooperate. This isn't easy, since nobody wants to get checkmated. In other words, you have to plan for checkmate.

The Basic Checkmates

The first thing you need to know when planning checkmate is just what a checkmate looks like. Therefore, here are a number of checkmates using the various pieces and pawns. All nonessential pieces and pawns are removed so you see just the pure checkmate. Even the White king is missing in most cases.

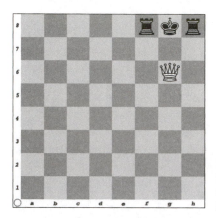

The queen covers the g-file as well as the seventh-rank escape squares. Black's rooks cover the other escape squares.

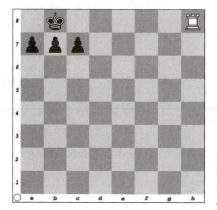

The rook covers all eighth-rank squares, while the seventh rank is denied to the king by his own pawns.

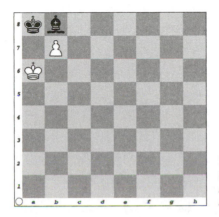

The White pawn checks, the White king takes away a7 and b7, and the Black bishop takes away b8.

The more you visualize checkmates like this one, the more adept you will be at finding a lurking opportunity any time there is a chance for one. Simply look for all the possible checks and determine if there is a way out. If not, you have found a checkmate!

DEFINITION

Basic checkmates are those produced with the minimum amount of material: The king getting checkmated and the king and piece or pieces needed to produce the checkmates are the only pieces occupying the board. There are no pawns in these basic checkmate positions. These include:

- Two rooks
- Rook and king
- Queen and king
- Two bishops and king
- Bishop, knight, and king

In only the first of the list, the one involving two rooks, is the strong side's king unnecessary. There is also queen and rook or two queens, but these are redundant. You will notice that two knights and king do not appear on the list. You can checkmate an inattentive opponent using only those pieces, but an experienced player will always be able to slip away. There is no way to force checkmate with only two knights and king against a lone king.

THREE STEPS TO CHECKMATE

Checkmates don't simply spring up on inspiration when you want them to. There are three steps to anticipate. The first step is to know what the checkmates look like. The next step is to find checkmates lurking on the very next move. The third and hardest phase is to recognize a checkmate pattern forming and then play to bring it about.

SOME EXAMPLES

Here are some positions where a checkmate waits to be found on the next move. All you have to do is find the right check. It is White to move and checkmate Black in each case.

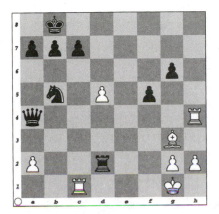

1. Rh8#.

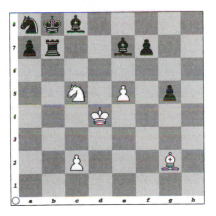

1. Na6#.

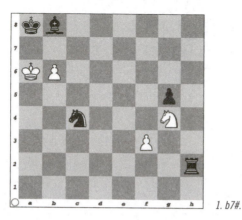

1. b7#.

Two Rooks

This is the simplest and the easiest to execute of the basic checkmates. It is the same whether we use two rooks, two queens, or rook and queen. The strong king isn't even necessary, and could get in the way if we aren't careful.

THE CHECKMATE

The final checkmate will have the weak king on the edge of the board. Either the a-file or h-file or the first rank or eighth rank will do. But don't think you can checkmate a king in the middle of the board unless he cooperates or you use your own king to help.

Lay the board out with the Black king on h8 and the White rooks on c8 and d7. The White king is on g1. Note that the checkmated king is on the edge of the board and that the rooks take away the seventh and eighth ranks.

The reason you need to herd the weak king to the side of the board or, even better, a corner of the board, is that he has too many escape squares when he is in the center. The weak king is hard to trap in the center just because he has so many possibilities. Naturally, any intelligent weak king is going to try to stay in or near the center in order to preserve his life, so your plan must be to induce him to the side or corner and checkmate him there.

THE PLAN

The lumbering giants can herd the king to the side of the board by what is sometimes referred to as *bicycle pedaling*. One full rank (or file) is first taken away from the weak king by one of the rooks. Then the next rank is taken away by the other rook, then the next by the first rook, until the poor beleaguered fellow reaches the edge of the board. At that time he has no further recourse and is checkmated.

Here's how it works:

Lay the board out with the white rooks on a1 and b1. The White king is on g1, and the Black king is on h5. Now the game continues: **1. Ra4 Kg5 2. Rb5+ Kf6 3. Ra6+ Ke7 4. Rb7+ Kd8 5. Ra8#.**

Rook and King

This is trickier and takes a little longer, but the checkmate is there if you know what you are doing. It will look something like this:

Lay out the board with the White king on f5 and the Black king on h5. The White rook is on h8. Once again, the checkmated king is on the edge of the board. The rook takes away the h-file, while the White king takes away the g-file.

You can see the same effect if you lay out the board so that the White rook is on a4, checking the Black king, which is on a8, while the White king keeps him in the corner, sitting on c7. The rook takes away the a-file, while the White king covers the b-file.

Finally, lay out the board with the White rook on c1, the Black king on e1, and the White king on e3. The rook covers the first rank while the White king takes away second-rank squares.

OPPOSITION

When two kings face each other on a rank or file, with a space in between, the person who doesn't have the move is said to have the opposition. You want to have the opposition because then you can boss the other king around.

The way to use it in king and king-versus-rook positions is to take an entire rank or file away from the opposing king using the opposition. Thus, your king fulfills the role of one of the rooks in the two-rook checkmate.

The idea of gradually taking squares away from the weak king is the whole key to this checkmate plan. The weapons you use are the opposition and the tremendous long-range power of the rook, which can take away an entire file or rank from the lone weak king, or lose a move in order to persuade that monarch to step into the opposition himself. When your prey is finally in jail, with nowhere left to go, it is time for the checkmate.

FOR FURTHER READING

There are many books devoted to checkmate and the endgame on the market. The simplest are those of A.J. Gillam, who fills his books with checkmate positions or positions one move from checkmate. Others include *Bobby Fischer Teaches Chess*, which is a step-by-step explanation of how to find the lurking checkmating patterns in positions two and three moves away from the final checkmate.

TAKING SQUARES AWAY

Here's how to do it. This is really nothing more than a slower way to execute the two-rook checkmate. It's just that your king isn't as powerful as the other rook was. So you have to use the opposition to take a rank or file away from the weak king.

Lay out your board with the White king on b4, the Black king on b6, and the White rook on f2. The kings are already in opposition.

1. Rf6+ Kc7 2. Kc5 Kd7.

Let's look at a situation in which the kings are not yet in opposition. Continue where the previous example ended with the White king on c5, the Black king on d7, and the White rook on f6. Now play:

3. Kd5 Ke7 4. Rf1.

This last move is the key. White does not move into the opposition. Rather, he gently persuades Black to move into the opposition himself by dropping back with his rook.

The Black king is about to step into the opposition again.

4. ... Kd7 5. Rf7+ Ke8 6. Ke6 Kd8.

White keeps the king confined.

7. Kd6 Ke8.

Black moves out of opposition again.

8. Rf2 Kd8.

And White administers the coup de grace:

9. Rf8#.

THE BACK-RANK MATE

The back-rank mate, also referred to as the *corridor mate*, is one that can be executed only by a major piece. It is the mate that ends the king and major piece against king positions. It can take place on a side file as well as a side rank. But it can also come

about when the next file or rank is denied the checkmated king by
something other than an enemy king and opposition. Following are
a couple of examples.

White checkmates with 1. Rf7.

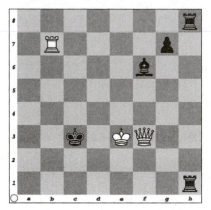

White checkmates with 1. Qc6.

Queen and King

Since a queen is more powerful than a rook, you would think that checkmating with king and queen would be easier than checkmating with king and rook. Well, yes, you can generally checkmate the lone king much faster with king and queen. But doing so is also trickier.

KING AND PAWN CHECKMATE

Since a lone rook and king can force checkmate against a lone king, and a lone queen and king can force checkmate against a lone king, it follows that a lone pawn and king can also force checkmate against a lone king—provided that the king and pawn can combine to force a safe promotion to a rook or queen.

STALEMATE!

The reason it is trickier to checkmate with a queen than with a rook is because the tremendous power of the queen often gives the weak king a chance to set up a stalemate trap. The best way to see that possibility is to try to checkmate a lone king with a lone queen. Nothing else is allowed on the board for this exercise—not even the strong king. You will soon find that, although the lone queen can push the lone king to the side of the board, there is never a checkmate. There are, however, stalemate opportunities.

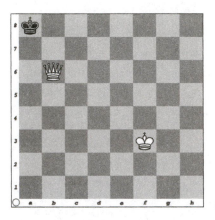

Black to move. Stalemate.

WITH THE KING'S HELP

Now add the strong king, and the stalemating opportunities go up! For instance:

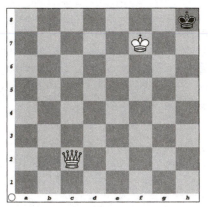

Black to move is stalemate.

So how can you avoid this sort of nasty stalemate? The best way to make sure you avoid stalemating a lone king is to be aware of the traps and look for them before making your move. Another way of avoiding these traps is to make sure your opponent's lone king has a spare square if you don't plan on placing him in check. A third way to avoid these traps is to remember that the queen is a long-range piece, and keep her far away.

THE CHECKMATES

Just as there are more stalemate possibilities with queen and king versus lone king, there are also more possible checkmates. Here is what one looks like:

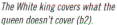
The White king covers what the queen doesn't cover (b2).

Practice king and major piece against king checkmates against your computer or a willing partner. Once you know them cold you can go into a position, even quite a complicated position, in which you have an extra pawn, and you already know a good plan of action:

1. Exchange off all the pieces.
2. Push your extra pawn through to promotion.

3. Use your king and new queen (or rook) to checkmate the lone king.

The Two Bishops

Checkmate can always be forced with king and major piece against lone king. Checkmate can never even come about with king and minor piece against lone king. But with king and two minor pieces against lone king, the situation is more complicated. The plan in all the basic positions involving king and two minor pieces against king is to drive the lone king into a corner of the board. Getting him to the edge just isn't enough.

THE CHECKMATE

The easiest checkmate to get with king and two minor pieces versus lone king is the one in which your two minor pieces are both bishops. Here you can checkmate the lone king in any corner of the board. The checkmate looks like this:

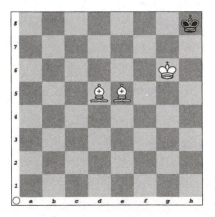

The e5 bishop delivers the check and covers g7. The d5 bishop takes away g8. The king takes away g7 and h7.

The plan in these endings is basically simple. Step 1 is to drive the lone king to the corner, by using both your bishops and your king to methodically take squares away from him. Step 2 is to make sure your bishops have enough room to operate. Step 3 is to get your king out of their way at the last minute.

WORKING IT OUT

Although the concept is simple enough, it is very tricky to use the three pieces together as a team. The bishop's power is subtler than that of the major pieces. Just try to checkmate a lone king using two bishops like you did with a lone queen, and you will soon see that it can't be done. So we will look at a checkmate using two bishops and king versus king, and work it out, move by move, to understand how it was done.

Place the White king on c3, the White bishop on d3, and the other White bishop on e3. Place the Black king on f6.

White to move. **1. Bf4.** Notice that the fifth rank is off-limits to the lone king, thanks to the bishops. **1. ... Ke6.**

2. Kd4. Now the strong king comes up to help. Notice that d6 is off-limits to Black. **2. ... Kd7.**

3. Kd5. Now the sixth rank and c7 are off-limits. **3. ... Ke7 4. Be5.**

The f6 escape square is taken away. **4. ... Kd7.**

5. Bf5+. Now much of the seventh rank is denied Black. **5. ... Ke7.**

6. Kc6. The bishops are perfectly placed, so White now brings his king closer. **6. ... Kf7. 7. Kd7 Kg8.** Alert! The Black king can only move to f7 or f8. Therefore, White will blow it by moving 8. Ke8 or 8. Ke7, both of which produce stalemate.

8. Ke6. Now Black has a square to go to: f8. **8. ... Kf8**

9. Bg6. White takes e8 away. **9. ... Kg8.**

This is another alert. The Black king has only f8 as an escape. Therefore, White must avoid 10. Ke7, which is a stalemate.

10. Kf6 Kf8. If Black plays 10. ... Kh8, we end it early with 11. Kf7#.

11. Bd6+ White drives the lone king to the corner. **11. ... Kg8.**

12. Be4. White gives himself some breathing room while not allowing the Black king out of his box. **12. ... Kh8.**

13. Kg6. The White king makes room for the bishops. **13. ... Kg8.**

14. Bd5+ Kh8.

15. Be5#.

Learning these king and two minor pieces versus king checkmates constitutes a very good course in basic chess strategy. All the principles you have learned and will learn in the future apply: Control the center, coordinate your pieces, use all the pieces, and make use of threats. Once you know these basic checkmates by heart, you will probably already be a pretty good chess player.

Bishop and Knight

This one is the hardest of the basic checkmates. That's because it is no longer good enough to force the lone king into a corner: It has to be the corner of the color of your bishop. You simply cannot produce a checkmate anywhere else.

THE CHECKMATE

The checkmates can take several forms. You can set them up on your board:

- Place the Black king on h8, the White bishop on f6, the White king on g6, and the White knight on h6. The bishop delivers the check. Knight and king act in supporting roles.
- Place the Black king on h8, the White knight on e7, the White bishop on g7, and the White king on g6. The bishop delivers the check. Knight and king act in supporting roles.
- Place the Black king on g8, the White bishop on g7, the White king on g6, and the White knight on f6. The knight delivers the check. Bishop and king act in supporting roles.

DRIVING THE KING

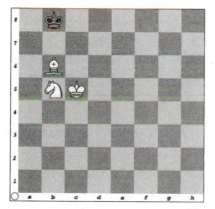

Here is a position well along the way to completion. You will notice that the lone king is very close to the wrong corner.

Phase one of this very complex checkmate is to drive the lone king to the edge of the board. In the diagram, that phase has already been completed.

Phase two is to drive the king toward the more friendly corner, and it is done like this:

1. Kc6. White confines the Black monarch to the eighth rank.

1. ... Ka8. If Black wants to cooperate by playing 1. ... Kc8, then White takes the b8 square away with 2. Ba7. But not 2. Bc7, which is a stalemate!

2. Nc7+. This move drives the king out of his comfy corner. Another stalemate is produced by 2. Bc7.

2. ... Kb8 3. Bc5. A big key to chess strategy is to not give anything up if you can help it. White keeps all the squares she has gained and prepares to take more away from Black.

3. ... Kc8 4. Ba7. Now we have the lone king traveling in the right direction.

4. ... Kd8 5. Nd5. Notice how all the White pieces cooperate in the effort to keep Black from gaining squares.

5. ... Kc8. Black tries to stay near his most comfortable corner. If he tries to go to the middle, he will wind up in the wrong corner anyway, like so: 5. ... Ke8 6. Kd6 Kf7 7. Bf2 Kg6 8. Ke5 Kg5 9. Nf6 Kg6 10. Ke6 Kg5 11. Bg3 Kg6 12. Bf4. Notice how White keeps using all three pieces to gradually take squares away from the slippery Black monarch.

6. Ne7+ Kd8 7. Kd6 Ke8 8. Ke6 Kd8 9. Bb6+ Ke8 10. Nf5 Kf8.

Now White should transfer the bishop to a more useful diagonal.

11. Bd8 Ke8 12. Bf6 Kf8 13. Be7+ Kg8. Of course, Black can always end it prematurely with 13. ... Ke8 14. Nd6#.

14. Kf6 Kh7 15. Kf7 Kh8. This is a tricky situation. Although the Black king is in the proper corner, it's premature to try to cash in, since there is no good follow-up after 16. Bf6+ Kh7.

16. Kg6 Kg8. Now we're ready for the final blow.

17. Nh6+ Kh8 18. Bf6#.

THE TWO KNIGHTS

This one is not possible except against a cooperative opponent. There simply is no way to force checkmate against a lone king when you have king and two knights. Incredible but true.

The only way to convince yourself of the truth of this statement is to try to do it. Any opponent who doesn't wish to get checkmated can simply head his king to the corner. There will always be a way out.

Other Checkmates

The basic checkmates are only a beginning. There are many, many checkmates possible—hundreds, thousands of them. Although it is impossible to go into detail on all the possibilities, not to mention the plans leading up to them, in an introductory work (or, for that matter, in a huge encyclopedia!), here is a smattering of various checkmates and a little on their history.

ARABIAN MATE

A rook and a supporting knight on the edge of the board cooperate in an Arabian mate.

This one is named after the early Arabian form of the game, before the queen and bishop had their current powers. Thus the strongest pieces in use were the rook and knight. The rook always produces this mate, and is defended by the knight, which also covers the king's escape square.

EPAULETTE MATE

The king wears these fringes, in the form of his own pieces or pawns, which take away his escape squares on either side. You can see what this looks like by placing the Black king on d8 and the Black rooks on either side of him, on c8 and e8. The White queen delivers the check from d6.

GUERIDON MATE

A *guéridon* is a small French café table. The king represents the tabletop, while the pieces or pawns diagonally behind him, which deny him those squares for escape, represent the table legs.

ANASTASIA'S MATE

Anastasia's mate is actually a special corridor or back-rank mate, with a rook delivering the mate, and the escape squares taken up by a friendly pawn and an enemy knight. To see what it looks like, place the Black king on h6, a Black pawn on g6, a White knight on e6, and the check-delivering White rook on h2.

This one is named after *Anastasia und das Schachspiel*, an 1803 novel by Wilhelm Heinse.

PHILIDOR'S LEGACY

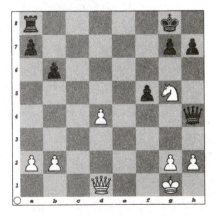

All the ingredients are here for a Philidor's legacy mate.

The ingredients include the open b3–g8 diagonal, a White queen able to get there with check, an exposed Black king on g8 with Black pawns on g7 and h7, the White knight on g5, a Black rook guarding the eighth rank, and complete White control over the f7 square. This is a form of smothered mate that Philidor first worked out in the eighteenth century. It goes like this:

1. Qb3+ Kh8. If 1. ... Kf8, White plays 2. Qf7#.

2. Nf7+ Kg8. Note that the Black king and the White queen are on the same diagonal. The only reason there isn't a check is that the White knight is in the way on the same diagonal. So White moves it out of the way with:

3. Nh6+.

A double check is extremely powerful. The only way out is to move the king.

3. ... Kh8. Now what?

4. Qg8+!!

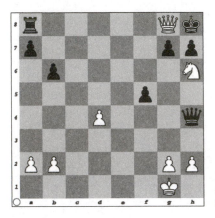

There is only one way to get out of check. Black must capture the rude intruder with his rook.

4. ... Rxg8 5. Nf7#.

The end result of a Philidor's legacy mate is always a smothered mate.

Who needs the queen when you have a knight that can do such great work?

SMOTHERED MATE WITH PIN

This one comes right out of the opening. In it, the White king is caught in the middle, surrounded by his own pieces and pawns. It goes like this:

1. d4 Nf6 2. c4 e5 3. dxe5 Ng4 4. Bf4 Bb4+ 5. Nd2 Nc6 6. Ngf3 Qe7 7. a3 Ncxe5.

Should White capture the bishop?

8. axb4 Nd3#. Looks like he should have left the bishop alone and defended his king instead!

The e2 pawn cannot capture the checking knight because that would expose the White king to the baleful eye of the Black queen.

Look for the Checks

To sum up, there are many ways to mate, but the art of winning is to be able to see through the pieces on the board to find those patterns. This is why, as we said earlier, one of the objects of the endgame is to simplify the board through exchanges of material. It is far easier to see a checkmate when extraneous pieces have been removed from play.

A final warning: Don't be so eager to find your own mate that you overlook threats from your opponent. She can see what you can see, and clearing the board offers her the same advantage that it does you. Guard against threats while seeking out lines of attack.

PART III

THE AMAZING WORLD OF CHESS

CHAPTER 11

The World of Competitive Chess

Now that you know how to play a reasonable game of chess, some new opportunities are waiting. There is a whole world out there built around the subculture that is chess. The following is just a sampling of what this chess world has to offer.

A Parlor Game

Chess is at its core simply a game between two players. A board and set is the only essential equipment, and even that can be dispensed with by those with enough imagination and concentration to play blind.

ANYWHERE

The game can be and is played virtually everywhere. At home, in a restaurant, coffee shop, library, or bar, outside in the park, on a train, and in the back seat of a car are a few places where a casual game can take place with no organization whatsoever.

Whether played in private or in public, such games are traditionally referred to as *skittles*. The chief difference between such casual chess and organized tournament games is a lack of time control, a lack of scorekeeping, and the danger of kibitzers.

WHAT IS A KIBITZER?

Literally an interfering onlooker, *kibitzers* are spectators who suggest moves to one or both of the contestants. This is illegal in any formal competition, of course, but is often tolerated in casual play. *Kibitzer* is a Yiddish word deriving from the German *Kiebitz*.

THE PARK

There are outdoor areas in city parks where chess is played daily, at least in the warmer months. Games can be timed or not, depending on the availability of clocks and the inclination of the players. You can play for stakes or merely for the sake of playing. Washington Square Park in New York City is famous for this, and was brought to the attention of the general public in the book and movie *Searching for Bobby Fischer*.

Chess Clubs

Between the informal games that anyone can play anywhere and serious tournament competition, there is what used to be the backbone of chess, the chess club.

Men's clubs of all types grew out of old-style intellectual gatherings. Eventually, these clubs began to specialize, and clubs devoted entirely to chess gained currency. At first, many of those clubs also included checkers and/or bridge as activities.

FAMOUS CHESS CLUBS

In the eighteenth and nineteenth centuries, the Café de la Régence in Paris was a famous meeting place for many of the day's intellectuals, and that included chess players. Other clubs, often of similar type, sprang up around Europe and, later, the United States. Such clubs were gathering places for people of diverse backgrounds and interests. They helped foster a common culture for their habitués.

Among the most famous American clubs are the Manhattan Chess Club, founded in 1877, and the Marshall Chess Club in the Greenwich Village neighborhood of New York City. It was at the latter club that in 1956 a thirteen-year-old Bobby Fischer played one of his most famous games, defeating International Master Donald Byrne.

CLUB ACTIVITIES

At a typical chess club, members and guests can find a casual game or get involved with whatever level of organized competition the club offers. *Ladder play*, where each member rises or falls in reference to other club members, used to be a popular way to keep track of everyone's progress, at least until ratings came into vogue. Besides regular blitz tournaments and the club championship, there is often league play, where each club in an area plays the other clubs throughout the course of a season. (During a *blitz tournament*, each player gets a total amount of time, say five minutes, to complete all the moves, so in a five-minute blitz the maximum time a game can take is ten minutes. This way, a round-robin tournament with fifteen to twenty players can finish in one night.)

SPEED CHESS

Blitz is one of several forms of speed chess. An even more intense game than the five-minute contest is one in which each player sets his clock for one minute, resulting in a total maximum game time of two minutes; some players claim to be able to look at the board, move their piece, and hit the button on the clock in under a second. Committed players often play hundreds, if not thousands, of speed chess games each year.

Some clubs have chess libraries available to members; some also provide access to chess lessons or lectures by the club pro or a visiting master. Some sponsor simultaneous exhibitions or tournaments. The variety and amount of service to members provided by any particular club is only subject to the dedication and energy of the people who run it.

THE DECLINE OF CLUBS

Late in the twentieth century the Swiss tournament took hold of the imagination of American chess players. A typical tournament usually took up an entire weekend and often involved some serious travel expenses.

Many players addicted to playing chess couldn't keep up all their club activities and play the tournament circuit. So these players would frequent weekend tournaments more and more, and their local clubs less and less.

This trend has continued with the advent of Internet chess play, where the club comes to the player rather than the other way around.

THE INTERNET AND CHESS

A pervasive part of modern society, the Internet brings like-minded people together and isolates them at the same time. Anyone with Internet access can now play a game of chess with a faceless opponent from anywhere on earth at any given hour, day or night. Thus both opponents get a game and communicate, but there is no face-to-face interaction.

Chess Instruction

Many people want to improve their results or learn more about the game. This can be accomplished in any number of ways, including:

- Reading instructional material.
- Playing strong opponents.
- Analyzing your own games.
- Attending lectures.
- Finding a chess teacher.
- Developing a plan that includes all of the previous bullets.

How far you take such instruction is entirely up to you. This book may be enough to allow you to enjoy chess as a hobby for the rest of your life. Or, you may want to improve enough to have a real chance to defeat a particular opponent or reach a particular rating. If you do decide to get serious about chess and wish to become a strong player or a champion, you will need to devote many years of striving to master the game.

MAKE A PLAN

A good plan for improving your chess play will include all the listed elements. Whether you study and compete face to face or via correspondence, use books and magazines, watch videos, find resources on the Internet, or purchase software is irrelevant. How much material you retain and use is much more to the point.

STRONG CHESS

Playing a strong game means understanding what is required in many different types of positions. Many players divide these types of positions into the various opening systems, endgames where there are very few pieces on the board, and middle-game structures where different strategies need to be mastered.

Others aim for types of positions that suit their personality. Do you like to attack? Then learn which positions will give you the chance to launch a successful attack. Do you prefer defense? Then learn how to set up a successful defensive structure and how to beat back the attacks your opponents will throw at you. Just remember that good defenders are rare. Or maybe you prefer to counterattack or prevent strong attacks altogether.

Whatever types of positions or style of play you prefer, you will have to find a way to learn to understand what the pieces and pawns should be doing in many different positions. That may involve memorizing many different opening variations, combination themes, and endgame positions. And you could get them all wrong. That's why a good chess teacher is probably the most important learning tool you can invest in.

FUN WITH CHESS

Most people who play chess do so for fun, without any aspirations of mastering the game. If that's you, none of this is too relevant. Find the level of competition you can handle, and play. Or, follow whatever chess news and/or games that interest you. If that's enough, you have a whole world of chess waiting for you.

Simultaneous Exhibitions

Picture a number of tables arranged in a rectangle or semicircle. There are chessboards on all the tables and people sitting in chairs along the outside, at each board. They are all playing chess. But where is their opponent?

Someone is walking along the inner side of the tables, going from board to board, making moves. This is the chess master, and she is playing everybody else at the same time.

It's quite a spectacle. Usually the master will win many if not most of the games, and will lose very few, if any. Sometimes the master does this with a blindfold on. The players call out their moves, and the master calls out the response.

The number of opponents one master can handle in this way depends on the space available and the amount of players she can attract. Anywhere from two or three to hundreds of boards have been accommodated. More usual is between ten and fifty.

BLINDFOLD CHESS

Many serious players regard blindfold chess as a kind of parlor trick—not really legitimate chess. Still, it's an impressive feat of memory. The blindfolded player calls out her moves, and someone else moves the pieces on the board, before which the challenger is seated. Some people have been able to play simultaneous games blindfolded. In the eighteenth century the great chess player François-André Danican Philidor was able to play up to three games at once while blindfolded, holding all the positions on the boards in his head.

NUMBERS

Statistics are sometimes kept on simultaneous exhibitions, particularly if the master plays blind. World records have even been claimed for simultaneous games. But such exhibitions take a lot of time to complete, and some opponents leave before their games have gone very far. Those unfinished games are scored as another number for the master, and are usually claimed as a win as well.

RECORD HOLDERS

Karl Podzielny played 575 games simultaneously in 1978. In 30½ hours he won 533, drew twenty-seven, and lost fifteen. Vlastimil Hort played 550 opponents, 201 simultaneously, and lost only ten games in 1977. The late George Koltanowski played fifty-six consecutive (not simultaneous) blindfold games, winning fifty and drawing six, in San Francisco in 1960.

TANDEM SIMULS

Sometimes more than one master may be in the middle of a simultaneous exhibition. In such a case (a *tandem simul*), each one only plays every second or third move. This can provide a nice chance for the amateur opponents, since the masters may have different styles and thus trip each other up.

Another type of tandem simul occurs when there are multiple simultaneous exhibitions going on at the same time. This is a common occurrence in chess camps, and happens each year on the East Coast with the famous annual "Chessathon," where scores of masters volunteer to play hundreds of schoolchildren.

Composed Problems

Some people in the chess world have nothing to do with playing games. These are the people interested in composing or solving chess *studies*, or composed problems.

Instead of beginning with the starting position, where the object of the game is to checkmate the opponent's king or at least prevent your own king from getting checkmated, such studies begin with whatever pieces and pawns the composer wants. There is a stipulation accompanying such studies, such as White to play and checkmate Black in two moves (or in six moves, or any number of moves).

The appeal of such exercises is an aesthetic one. Solvers are testing themselves against the position, not against an opponent. And composers are trying to express something beautiful in the way the pieces cooperate with each other.

Set up the following problem for yourself: Place the White king on h7, the White queen on g6, and the White rook on d3. Now place the Black king on a1, the Black bishop on b1, one Black pawn on b2, and another Black pawn on e5. White to move and mate in two moves.

This composition features the pin and the unpin. It is composed by V. Chepizhny and won first prize in the Nikolaev-200 competition in 1989. It appeared in the May 2000 issue of *Chess Life*, submitted by columnist Robert Lincoln. Solution: **1. Qg1.**

And not 1. Rd1, when 1. ... Ka2 escapes the pin and the mate, though 1. ... e4, with an unpin, succumbs to 2. Qa6#.

1. ... Ka2 2. Qa7# or 1. ... e4 (with an unpin) 2. Ra3#.

BUILDING CHESS VOCABULARY

The chess-problem world has specialized terms, such as self-block (a situation in which a player is forced to block squares with its own pieces that eventually enable his opponent to force checkmate), interference, battery (a formation of two pieces or more on the same line, with at least one of them a long-range piece), and excelsior (a problem in which a pawn starts out on its original square and takes either five or six moves to promote; the promotion, whether to a queen or an underpromotion, will produce checkmate).

ENDGAME STUDIES

These are a bit different than composed problems in that there is no forced checkmate in so many moves. Also, there are usually fewer pieces on the board. The stipulation is usually White to move and win or draw.

Here is an example of an endgame study: Place the White king on g1 and a White pawn on b2. Place the Black king on a5, one Black pawn on b6, and another on b7. White to play and draw.

This one was composed by Grigoriev in 1935 and appeared in Pal Benko's column in the April 2002 issue of *Chess Life*.

Solution: **1. Kf2 Ka4 2. Ke3 b5 3. Ke4!! Kb4 4. Kd4 Kb3 5. Kd5! b4 6. Kc5 b6+ 7. Kb5** and the position is drawn.

Other moves by White lead to the same position. For instance, 2. ... Kb3 3. Kd4 or 2. ... Kb4 3. Kd3.

HELPMATES

These compositions are completely strange to any chess competitor. Both sides, White and Black, cooperate in checkmating Black. And Black moves first.

Here is an example: Place one White knight on d1 and the other White knight on b1. Place the White king on a5. Place a Black bishop on a1, the Black king on a2, and a Black pawn on c2.

Helpmate in two; two solutions.

This one was composed by J. Boggio and appeared in *Europe Echecs* in 1962 and in *Chess Life* in September 2002.

In the solutions, you will note that Black's move is given first. It looks strange for a Black move to be recorded first, but helpmates are strange to begin with.

Solution 1: **1. cxb1=R Ka4 2. Rb2 Nc3#.**

Solution 2: **1. cxd1=N Kb4 2. Nb2 Nc3#.**

The themes of underpromotion, self-block, and interference predominate.

Serious Competition

If casual play or simuls or problems are not to your liking, or if they are not enough, there's always serious competition to be had, either in some rated tournament or match.

SWISS-SYSTEM TOURNAMENTS

In the United States, structured competition outside the club became quite big in the latter half of the twentieth century. This came with the introduction of the Swiss-system tournament, which allows every competitor to play five or six games in a weekend. In a Swiss-system tournament, you play opponents with a score the same as yours, or very similar to it, throughout the event.

MATCHES

This was always and still is the essence of chess. You and me: Let's find out who plays better chess.

A match between two strong players that is rated and sanctioned and followed by fans can be exhilarating. But you don't have to be a champion or even a very strong player to get a similar exhilaration. All you need is a willing opponent somewhere close to your own strength.

If you want an audience, set up your match at a mall or an outdoor festival. If you'd rather just slug it out in private, somebody's home, or perhaps the library, is good enough. All you really need is an appropriate opponent who is willing to engage you in the match.

BE ON TIME!

For any scheduled chess game, it is important to show up on time. Failure to do so is not only rude; it also could damage your chances in the game. In a timed encounter, your clock begins ticking when the game is scheduled. If you fail to show up in the next hour, you forfeit the game.

TOURNAMENTS

Formal tournaments come in various types, and most people are familiar with at least several of those types. Tournaments are held in many sports and games, including Scrabble, bridge, and tennis.

The types of tournaments used for chess tournaments include:

1. Round robin
2. Double round robin
3. Knockout
4. Swiss system

The round robin is a very basic device that can handle a few people in a short time or a lot of people over a long period of time. Every competitor plays every other competitor. If there are eight players, each will play seven games.

Another version of the round robin is the double round robin. Each player gets a game with White and a game with Black, with every other competitor. This way, nobody has any inherent advantage. The obvious disadvantage is that playing two games against each of your seven opponents means playing fourteen games. And that may take a long time.

The round robin and especially the double round robin have comprised the staple of professional chess for a long time. But such tournaments typically take a few weeks to a month to complete, especially when professionals insist on playing only one game a day.

Most people simply don't have the time or the resources or the energy to go through such a brutal schedule. So the alternate systems are much more appropriate for the casual player or even the serious amateur.

If you are familiar with the knockout system, this probably comes from watching tennis. You play until you lose. At the end, only one player remains as the champion. This is an exciting type of tournament, but hasn't really caught on in the chess community.

The tournament of choice for most chess players in the United States is the Swiss system, which is essentially a knockout format with nobody getting eliminated. If you lose, you simply play someone else who has lost. But it resembles a knockout for the winner.

RANKING

Ranking is important for a Swiss-system tournament. Based on each player's ratings, they are divided into two groups for the first round. The top-ranked player in the top group plays the top-ranked player in the bottom group, the second player in the first group plays the second player in the bottom group, etc. In subsequent rounds, the players are divided up by score group. In the third round, all those with three wins are in one group, those with two and a half wins comprise the next score group, those with two another, etc. Each score group is divided in two, with the top player from the top group playing the top player from the bottom group.

Correspondence Chess

Playing chess through the mail is not an activity for impatient people. A game can take over a year to complete, with moves coming on a weekly basis.

But correspondence in general is mostly a faded memory of what it used to be, and correspondence chess is no exception. Our modern world includes TV, radio, telephone, e-mail, and the Internet. These have all eroded our need for correspondence, but have also provided us with alternate ways to communicate. Thus there are telephone, e-mail, and Internet chess competitions, as well as the more traditional face-to-face and correspondence-by-mail games. (These are as opposed to over-the-board (OTB) tournaments in which players face one another across the chess board.)

CORRESPONDENCE TOURNAMENTS

There are sanctioned correspondence tournaments where you pay a fee and can earn a prize. These events are rated, just like OTB tournaments. There are arbiters, or referees, to make sure the event runs smoothly and everyone sends in their moves on time.

Of course, chess notation is what makes correspondence chess possible. You simply write your move on a letter or postcard and send it off. It's a good idea to include the last couple of moves, and even a diagram if you can. And it's also a good idea to keep a separate board handy that has the current position on it. This is especially true if you have more than one game going.

Chess Books and Magazines

A huge number of chess books and magazines are available to the enthusiast. It has been claimed that there are more books on chess than on all other subjects combined. And more are being written every day.

SUBJECT MATTER

These books cover a bewildering array of chess material. Their subject matter can range from spot the checkmate and find the combination themes, to pamphlets and even large tomes devoted to a subvariation of just one of type of opening. They can focus on explanations of how to handle isolated pawn positions or offer collections of some of the great games. There are books devoted to endgame studies or historical changes in style. Somewhere along the way, every conceivable area of the game is covered.

POPULARITY OF OPENINGS

The most popular chess books in the United States are those on openings. Whether they're multivolume reference works that cover all the main openings, or specialty books that cover the latest trends in certain variations, or how-to texts on specific openings or variations, these opening books are in great demand.

MAGAZINES

Besides the official national chess magazine, *Chess Life*, there are official state magazines for practically every state, correspondence chess magazines, problem magazines, even a blitz chess magazine! With resources like that, you will never run out of reading material. This doesn't include the various club bulletins and local publications that come and go. And we haven't even touched on the Internet yet. There are also extensive online resources, ranging from posts of players in search of games, to instructional blogs, to sites on which to practice your chess moves. You can find links to many of these sites *at www.kenilworthchessclub.org/links/instructional.html* and *www.mashable.com/2007/09/23/chess-toolbox/*.

Chess in Education

There is a concerted effort these days to get chess into primary and secondary schools, either as an afterschool activity or as a required subject. Some school administrators and teachers have become convinced that the act of learning chess increases cognitive skills and self-esteem.

There have been several studies done, using scientific criteria, to determine what learning chess can do for students. If these studies are accurate, the unmistakable conclusion is that when students learn chess, they learn to make decisions, plan ahead, accept the consequences of their decisions, think analytically, and thus improve self-esteem.

These studies have taken place using grade-school students as the subjects, and they have taken place among privileged subjects as well as at-risk subjects. The results are always the same. Whether rich or poor, whether taken from prosperous families or socially and/or financially challenged ones, students who learn chess seem to improve their thinking skills.

TRANSFERABLE SKILLS

Another reason chess in the schools is such a good idea is the great amount of transferability involved. Skills learned through chess can transfer to skills in math, geography, English, foreign languages, science, finance, art, and many other subjects.

Other Forms of Chess

There are other games that use most of the rules of chess and the same equipment. Some of these are popular, and some have been almost forgotten. Others are being invented as you read.

BUGHOUSE

Very popular with the younger crowd, this version of chess requires two boards, two sets, and four players. It is real team chess, with each team consisting of two players. One plays White on one board while the other plays Black on the other board. When a piece or pawn is captured, it does not simply leave the board. It becomes the property of your teammate. When you have acquired extra pieces or pawns in this way, you can use one of them by placing it anywhere on the board (with certain restrictions) in place of making a normal move.

CHESS VARIANTS

There are thousands of chess variants, ranging from three-dimensional chess to versions that add squares to the board and pieces to the set. Older versions also exist, such as Chinese chess and Japanese chess, which are closer to the original Indian or Persian game. But none of them has garnered the great popularity of the royal game that we all know.

FISCHER RANDOM

One of the most widespread variants is called *Shuffle Chess*, in which the pieces are randomized in their starting locations. All the pieces are still placed on the first and eighth ranks, but not in the normal order.

The most famous version of Shuffle Chess was created by Bobby Fischer in 1996. Initially named Fischer Random, it is now known as Chess960, since there are 960 possible starting positions. Fischer's intent was to minimize the value of prepared openings, making it easier for lower-ranked players to compete against higher-ranked ones.

Another, similar, idea is called *prechess*. The game begins with only the pawns on the board, and each player's first eight moves consist of placing his pieces somewhere on the first rank (for White) or the eighth rank (for Black). The bishops must occupy opposite color squares.

The reason for these variations is simply that openings have been studied so intensely for the last couple hundred years, many players feel this tremendous body of knowledge takes away any possible creativity in the openings.

GIVEAWAY

In this version, the object of the game is not checkmate. Rather, it is to give away every piece and pawn. Besides being able to ignore check and checkmate with impunity, the other peculiarity of *giveaway chess* is that captures are mandatory.

CHAPTER 12

Famous Matches and Players

What's the most famous game of chess ever played? That's an almost impossible question. Every serious chess player has an opinion on the *best* game ever, as well as the best player.

The world of grandmasters is so rarified that there are only a handful of contenders for the title of best chess player. Certainly there is a small group that profoundly influenced how the game is played. This elite includes:

- Alexander Alhekine (1892–1946)
- Mikhail Botvinnik (1911–1995)
- José Capablanca (1888–1942)
- Magnus Carlsen (1990–)
- Bobby Fischer (1943–2008)
- Vasily Ivanchuk (1969–)
- Anatoly Karpov (1951–)
- Garry Kasparov (1963–)
- Vladmir Kramnik (1975–)
- Paul Morphy (1837–1884)

- Tigran Petrosian (1929–1984)
- Judit Polgár (1976–)
- Boris Spassky (1937–)
- Wilhelm Steinitz (1836–1900)
- Mikhail Tal (1936–1992)
- Veselin Topalov (1975–)

Although there is no space here to discuss all of these distinguished players, a few deserve special mention.

Wilhelm Steinitz

Steinitz can claim to be the first World Chess Champion, a position he held from 1886 to 1894. He was also one of the first and most influential people to study and write about the game. Steinitz's game was a development of positional chess, a style in which the player tries to gain short-term advantages through attacks rather than developing long strings of preplanned moves. This style had already been developed by players such as Paul Morphy, but Steinitz took it further, to an extraordinary degree. He created a kind of chess that critics dubbed "scientific."

Unfortunately, along with his brilliance as a player came mental instability. A sufferer from insomnia and mounting psychoses, Steinitz was, for a time, confined to an insane asylum. There, he assured interviewers, he had defeated God in a game of chess, played over an invisible telephone wire. (Sadly, Morphy also suffered from delusions and died at age forty-seven.)

Although there is some debate among chess scholars today as to whether Steinitz's style of play would hold up against modern masters, he seems to have had little trouble holding his own against his contemporaries. In a famous match against Curt von Bardeleben in Hastings, England in 1895, Steinitz humiliated his opponent. After playing the Giuoco Piano opening (literally, the *quiet opening*), Steinitz kept up pressure on his opponent. On the twenty-second move of the match he opened the line for a possible rook sacrifice, which would have placed Bardeleben in an impossible position. On the twenty-fourth move, he pinned Bardeleben's queen to his rook. Bardeleben, in disgust, neglected to even resign and simply left the hall, handing Steinitz the game. The game was later dubbed "The Battle of Hastings" after the famous military conflict in 1066 in which the Normans defeated the Anglo-Saxons.

Judit Polgár

The strongest female chess player in the world comes from an unusual family and is the result of an unusual experiment. In the latter part of the 1960s, a Hungarian psychologist, Laszlo Polgár, announced that anyone could be trained to become a genius and that he intended to demonstrate this by training his children intensively in several disciplines, including chess. He and his wife had, as it turned out, three girls: Zsuzsa, Zsófia, and Judit. True to his word, their father set them a strict regimen. Soon all the girls were studying chess eight to ten hours every day. Not terribly surprisingly, they became highly accomplished at the game. At twenty-one Zsuzsa (Susan) earned the title grandmaster, the first woman in history to do so. Judit outperformed her sister in 1991 at age fifteen, breaking the record previously set by Bobby Fischer for the youngest grandmaster in the history of chess.

HOUSEHOLD OF GENIUS

In 1993 Bobby Fischer, then on the run from the U.S. government for breaking State Department rules about travel to Yugoslavia and for unpaid back taxes, was invited by the Polgárs to stay with them for a time. (It was often an uncomfortable visit, since Fischer occasionally launched into anti-Semitic rants in front of his Jewish hosts.) The sisters all played chess with Fischer, but yielding to his demands they played only Fischer Random.

Although not formally crowned female World Chess Champion, Judit Polgár, on the basis of her rating and her string of defeats handed to top world players, is generally recognized as the strongest female player in the world. She is the only woman ever to be ranked among the planet's top ten chess players. Garry Kasparov said of her, "If to 'play like a girl' meant anything in chess, it would mean relentless aggression."

Among her significant games was a contest in 1996 against Alexei Shirov. The game was part of a tournament in which players were required to use the Open Sicilian opening. This is an opening that creates a strong center. Polgár succeeded in breaking Shirov's lines and had opened attacks along the king's side. On move 16 she unleashed a shattering attack on White's king and queen.

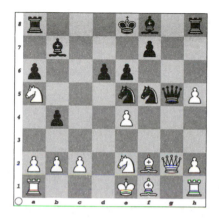

From this position Polgár played **16. ...Ne3.** If Shirov were to reply with Qxg5, then Nf3 produces mate for Black. If he answers Polgár with 17. Bxe3, then Polgár can reply with 17. ...Qxe3, and ultimately wins Black's queen. Shirov continued to play, but he was increasingly cramped and resigned after the twenty-ninth move. The game is a useful reminder of something we discussed back in the chapter on tactics: two knights placed together on the board are a powerful weapon.

Kasparov and Karpov

The history of chess, like the history of anything, is full of what ifs. One of the greatest is, What if Bobby Fischer, after winning the World Chess Champion title from Borris Spassky in 1972 at Reykjavik, had remained an active player in world chess circles? What would he have made of some of the up-and-coming players?

In particular, how would he have matched up against two of the most well-known players of the late twentieth century, Garry Kasparov and Anatoly Karpov?

Sadly, we'll never know the answer. After his victory over Spassky, Fischer largely isolated himself. He only re-emerged twenty years later to play his old foe and sometime friend Spassky in a rematch that netted him $3.5 million, which he badly needed.

PARANOIA AND MADNESS

In playing Spassky in 1992, Fischer traveled to war-torn Yugoslavia in defiance of direct instructions from the U.S. State Department. A warrant was issued for his arrest. After moving around to various locations in Europe, he settled on Iceland as his choice of country and was granted citizenship. His bitterness toward the United States took many forms, among them a hateful rant after the 2011 terrorist attacks in which he declared he wanted "to see the U.S. wiped out."

Fischer refused to defend his title in 1974 in a planned match with Karpov and was declared to have forfeited the title to the Russian. For a time he held the record for most consecutive tournament victories, until Kasparov passed him.

The degree to which Karpov and Kasparov were well-balanced against one another was illustrated by their most famous match, which began in September 1985. The victor had to win six games. Karpov swiftly built an impressive 4–0 lead, but Kasparov succeeded in drawing the next seventeen games. He lost one more game and drew the next nine before winning. There were a further fourteen draws before Kasparov won two more games. At this point, the head of the International Chess Federation stepped in and declared the contest over. The match had lasted for forty-eight games with no clear winner.

WORLD CHESS CHAMPIONSHIP 1985

When the two players met in Moscow the following year, the chess federation limited the match to twenty-four games. Whoever was ahead at the end of that would be declared the winner.

After fifteen games, the scores of the players were even (remember that in tournament play, players score 1 point for a win, ½ point for a draw, and 0 points for a loss). Incredibly, the match came down to game twenty-four. After a hard-fought battle in which Karpov sought to open lines of attack on Kasparov's king early in the game, Kasparov struggled back, and Karpov resigned on move 42.

Deep Blue

Kasparov was now World Chess Champion and one of the undisputed best players in the world. In 1996 he traveled to Philadelphia to undertake something new for him. He would play a computer specially designed to play chess; the match would occur under normal time controls (forty moves in two hours).

Deep Blue played the White pieces. The opening moves, in which Kasparov played the Sicilian Defense, were not unusual. Set up a board and play through the game.

1. e4 c5 2. c3 d5 3. exd5 Qxd5 4. d4 Nf6 5. Nf3 Bg4 6. Be2 e6 7. h3 Bh5 8. 0-0 Nc6 9. Be3 cxd4 10. cxd4 Bb4.

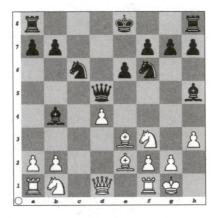

Kasparov in this last move is trying to find a new way to develop his bishop.

11. a3 Ba5 12. Nc3 Qd6 13. Nb5 Qe7?! 14. Ne5! Bxe2 15. Qxe2 0-0 16. Rac1 Rac8 17. Bg5

White has now pinned Black's knight on f6, a situation that can be traced back to Black's decision to develop the queen's bishop on the king's side.

17. ...Bb6 18. Bxf6! gxf6 19. Nc4! Rfd8 20. Nxb6! axb6 21. Rfd1 f5 22. Qe3! Qf6 23. d5!

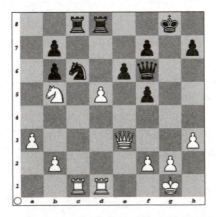

Note two things at this point: First, Black's pieces are being steadily pushed back and crowded away from the center of the board. Second, and perhaps more important, the placement of White's queen on the e3 square gives her formidable control over two diagonals (e3–h6 and e3–a7) as well as a commanding position in regard to the center.

At this point in the game, Deep Blue's advantages were overwhelming. The game continued along these lines:

23. ... Rxd5 24. Rxd5 exd5 25. b3! Kh8!? 26. Qxb6 Rg8 27. Qc5 d4? 28. Nd6 f4 29. Nxb7.

It's an instinct (if you can call it that) of chess-playing computers that when they see an opportunity to grab material and by doing so don't expose themselves to any immediate threat, they'll take it. Deep Blue takes a pawn here merely for the material advantage, not for any strategic reason.

29. ...Ne5 30. Qd5 f3 31. g3 Nd3 32. Rc7 Re8 33. Nd6 Re1+ 34. Kh2 Nxf2 35. Nxf7+ Kg7 36. Ng5+ Kh6 37. Rxh7+ 1-0.

And Kasparov resigns. Note that at the end, the checks from Deep Blue come fast and furious.

Match and Rematch

Although Kasparov lost the first game to the computer, he went on to win the match 4–2. After engineers reprogrammed the computer, it played Kasparov again in 1997. This time the computer won the match 3½–2½. Deep Blue (or "Deeper Blue" as the 1997 version was dubbed) thus became the first instance of a computer defeating a reigning World Chess Champion. Commentators jumped all over this as a sign that artificial intelligence had finally surpassed human intelligence. The jury is still out on that claim—on the whole, it seems we're a ways away from the benevolent reign of our computer overlords. But it's an interesting comment on the place of chess in our world that the measure of intelligence—human and computer—was a chess match.

Computerized Chess and Online Resources

Twenty or more years ago, when IBM produced the first computers, did we ever think that one day we'd be playing chess on a computer? Probably not. But technology, being what it is, has found a way to give us what we want, right in the palm of our hands.

A Modern Invention

Considering that chess started around A.D. 600, and computers only came on the scene a mere four to five decades ago, it might seem that chess and computers wouldn't mix. The modern invention of a computer that can play against people, play itself, analyze games, and run software that can teach you chess proves that the two go together surprisingly well. But, using artificial intelligence (AI), can computers really a match a person's ability to think through complicated moves to the finish? Realistically, computers are only as smart as they are programmed to be.

DAVID LEVY'S CHALLENGE

Back in 1970, when computers were first starting to play chess, International Master David Levy issued a £10,000 challenge to any programmer, stating that no computer could defeat him in a match within ten years. He later collected on his bet, defeating the best program of the day. He renewed the bet, and again collected, this time in 1990 versus Hans Berliner's computer, Deep Thought. But by then the computers were starting to offer real resistance, and he did not renew the challenge the third time.

FRITZ VERSUS THE WORLD

In October 2002, humanity got a measure of revenge for Kasparov's defeat by Deeper Blue when Braingames World Chess Champion Vladimir Kramnik played an eight-game match with Fritz, the strongest computer available. The match ended in a tie, with Kramnik winning two early games and Fritz rallying to win two late games. The other four games were drawn.

Machines That Play Chess

Everything from a mainframe, such as IBM's Deep Blue, to the smallest handheld devices can be programmed to play chess. If you want to go beyond the world of Internet chess, and take your chess game with you everywhere you go, you can now do so with the advent of smartphone chess apps and other portable types of handheld devices that feature chess games.

Some apps and devices are programmed to talk to you. They may offer advice to help you play better or snide comments, depending on the humor of the programmer. Such programs show a clear intent to replace your usual human opponent. As such, they will never succeed. But isn't it amazing what these machines can do?

Software That Plays Chess

There are many, many software programs that can be loaded into your computer, your handheld, or these days, your smartphone, that will allow you to play chess against a machine.

CHESS SOFTWARE

Among the software chess aficionados can buy today is Chess King with Houdini. Version 4 includes a 6 million game database, multiple levels of play, analysis tools, and more. There's also Fritz Chess 14, available as a download and including a database of more than 1.5 million games and hours of instruction. And, of course, there are numerous websites with online resources for chess (see Chapter 11).

Most available packages have something of everything: a database of games, the ability to play you or itself, the ability to analyze each move and give the results of its analysis. You can probably learn more sitting at your computer for a couple hours than you ever could simply reading a chess book. It's the interactive part that is such a wonderful coaching device.

FOCUS

Other software includes programs that focus specifically on tutorials, or on games played by grandmasters with their notes so you can study their moves. Still others offer specific opening, middle-game, and endgame sequences, as well as specific strategies and tactics such as the Dragon and Najdorf variations of the Sicilian Defense. Many computer software programs have an extensive library of games, and allow you to download other, newer games to your computer or device.

Analysis Engines

If you want to analyze your games, or the games of another, analysis engines rank at the top in allowing you to separate out every move and decide whether or not it was a good one. In addition, analysis engines will even suggest other moves that you might have made instead.

But you must beware. Computers still have a different way of "looking at" positions than humans do. Psychological considerations don't come into their thoughts at all, and humans often need this element in order to play well.

Also, the computers are not perfect yet. They still evaluate positions where one side has a lot of material as a win for that side unless there is a forced sequence of moves ending in checkmate for the side with the lesser material. And sometimes that sequence of moves is there, but it is too far off in the future for the analysis engine to pick up on it.

ALERTS

When purchasing a chess-playing app or an analysis engine, make sure it is compatible with your operating system. Make sure you know that these are minimum requirements. It is usually better to have more capabilities than you need.

Online Chess

The Internet has opened up a whole new world of gaming. If you want to play chess with someone, but can't or won't do it in a face-to-face tournament, or you aren't a fan of correspondence chess, then the Internet offers so many possibilities for engaging in your pastime.

It's becoming so popular for people to play chess over the Internet that new sites spring up each day. There are numerous web-based sites for different types of OTB (over-the-board) play. If you are at work, or at home working on your computer and you need a short diversion, a quick computer chess game can be just the thing for you.

CHESS COMPUTER ETIQUETTE

If you play online chess, it's considered bad form, and is also against the official rules and regulations, to use a computer to help you win. A game is supposed to be between two players, not two players with helpers. Policing this rule is a real challenge for Internet and correspondence tournament directors, as you might expect.

HOW CAN I PLAY ONLINE?

Internet chess play is an interactive way of playing OTB chess without having to leave the comfort of your home or office. As long as you have a connection to the Internet, you can play chess. That means that you can play in a car, on a plane, through your laptop, or at your desktop computer.

Different sites offer different things, but generally all sites offer interactive play, ratings, discussions groups, information on chess software, chess databases, and a place for further reading and study. In addition, you can usually get a rating after each game played, and many sites offer lectures with grandmasters and other top players. Visiting several sites to get a feel for the atmosphere and how chess is played there will help you decide which one is right for you.

INTERNET CHESS CLUBS

Chess games can be played in real time, similar to playing games of chess via telephone. Clubs also offer information and discussion about databases, games collections, chess-playing software, and other computer programs of a similar nature, either offered for sale, or in the state of development.

If you don't know where to look for a chess game, start with your favorite search engine. Type "chess games" in the search field, and watch what happens. You'll be presented with a myriad of sites that will allow you to play chess. Some charge a fee, some are for members only, and some may be free. But generally you can find a game twenty-four hours of the day, seven days a week.

Many sites allow you to play games using any time control you and your opponent agree to, ranging from one minute for the whole game to five or more hours. You can also get ratings, blitz, and slow chess. Each game is rated immediately after it is played, but if you prefer, you can play unrated games too.

A unique feature is that you can watch a variety of other players, use graphical interfaces that allow you to make your moves using a mouse or your fingertip (the old drag-and-drop technique), talk to anyone from around the world, or even participate in or watch simultaneous matches.

Internet Sources

As mentioned earlier, there are an unbelievable amount of chess sites out there in cyberspace.

ONLINE MAGAZINES AND NEWS GROUPS

If you like to read your information online, there's plenty of chess available. The list is so vast that it's impossible to list them all. Suffice it to say that each of the major chess sites have their own versions of online chess news to keep you up to date. And if you are playing chess online, you should be able to access news and information through these sources.

Some of the major sources include:

- USCF (*www.uschess.org*)
- New In Chess (*www.newinchess.com*)
- Chess & Bridge (*www.chess.co.uk*)
- The Week in Chess (*www.theweekinchess.com*)
- Europe Echecs (*www.europe-echecs.com*)

You can also download most popular chess software and learn about other computers playing online. Additionally, you should be able to find and play in tournaments, view others' games, visit with top-rated players on special events and online talks, and view your standings. Many sites also have chess experts who are willing to devote their time and effort to help beginning chess players to improve their game.

CHESS GAMES ONLINE

If you are looking to play casual chess online, it's best to go to one of the general game sites. However, if you are looking for hard-core chess, you'll want to check out specific chess gaming sites such as the site for the U.S. Chess League (*www.uschessleague.com*) or the Internet Chess Club (*www .chessclub.com*). They run tournaments and many other feature events, and are populated with many strong and famous players.

SOME FEATURES

Diagrams, commentary on games, news, politics, and more are included on many sites. In addition, you can also see live coverage of many scholastic and national and international championships. In many cases you can see the games as they are being played and you may also be able to hear a grandmaster commentary on the play-by-play. Also, each week interesting articles, interviews, chess problems, and all of the games of significant tournaments are published and posted to various sites.

Internet chess clubs are also a great way to get information about chess books and equipment. If you can't make a decision about which book to purchase or which computer chess game is better for your kid, then you can read more about the product online, or you can ask the experts.

TYPES OF EVENTS

Many people are familiar with the famous game played by Garry Kasparov against the world. This was an online chess game held in 1999. Microsoft sponsored the event, Kasparov had White, and his opponent (the world) had Black. Anyone could go to the website and register a single vote for a chess move. Whichever move won the vote would be played against Kasparov. Each side had one day to play a move.

Kasparov had a rough time with this game. There were several professional chess players who offered their advice to the world, so the move that won turned out to be quite good. Kasparov was surprised out of the opening and so the game became a real fight. In fact, the world could have drawn an endgame, but there was disagreement over which move to play, and the wrong move won. Kasparov was triumphant. But the game was, perhaps, an indication that the face of chess continues to change. What will it be like in another hundred years? No one can say.

Glossary

adjust

A player, when it is his turn to move, may adjust a piece (slide it to the center of the square) by first announcing "J'adoube" or "I adjust."

attack

Any of various ways to try breaking down your opponent's defense.

back-rank mate

This is a mate that occurs on any row (rank or file) at the edge of the board.

battery

Any two long-range pieces of the same color lined up along one line of attack.

bishop

A piece that moves on diagonals, any number of squares, and starts out next to the king and queen. Each player gets two: one that travels on light-square diagonals, and one that travels on dark-square diagonals.

Black

The dark pieces are referred to as Black in chess, regardless of their actual color.

blindfolded chess

A game of chess that is played by one or both opponents without the sight of a board and pieces.

capture

A pawn or piece may be captured (taken) when an opponent's piece may legally move to the square the pawn or piece occupies.

castling

A player moves the king two squares to the right or left toward one of his rooks. The rook is then moved to the opposite side of the king and placed on the adjacent square. Neither piece may have moved before, and the king may not castle into, out of, or through check.

center

It is important to fight for control of the center of the board. Central development allows for greater mobility and space for the pieces.

check

A move that places the king under attack.

checkmate

When the king is under attack and there is no legal way to get the king out of check.

chess clock
A device with two clocks connected to keep track of each individual's time during a chess game.

chess computer
A computer dedicated solely to playing chess.

chess etiquette
The rules of conduct that govern chess play. These rules of conduct are good manners, but also laws of chess.

chessboard
A checkered board with sixty-four squares in an eight-by-eight arrangement.

combination
A series of moves combining tactical weapons to gain an advantage.

convergence
Any two or more pieces or pawns of the same color lined up to threaten an enemy square, piece, or pawn.

coordinate squares
An endgame situation in which certain squares are linked to other squares. When the enemy king goes to one square, your king must be able to get to its corresponding square.

defense
Various ways to hold back or neutralize your opponent's threats.

desperado
A tactic in which a piece or pawn that is lost in any case captures an enemy piece or pawn to take along with it.

development
Moving the pieces from their starting squares, usually toward the center of the board. This is the major goal of the opening.

discovered attack
A surprise attack created when one piece moves and uncovers an attack by another piece on the same rank, file, or diagonal.

discovered check
A type of discovered attack that places the king in check.

double attack
A situation in which two or more enemy squares, pieces, and/or pawns are threatened simultaneously.

double check
A discovered check that attacks the king with two pieces.

draw
A tie game. No one wins.

en passant
A French term that means "in passing." When one player moves a pawn two squares to try to escape capture by the opponent's pawn, the pawn is captured *in passing* as though it had only moved one square.

en prise

From the French, meaning "in take." A piece is en prise when it is under attack and undefended.

endgame

The portion of the game in which so many pieces have been captured that the kings can take an active part in the battle.

Exchange

A term for the trading of a rook for a minor piece, such as winning a rook for a bishop or a knight. Such a trade is called *winning the Exchange*.

fianchetto

From the Italian, development of a bishop to b2, g2, b7, or g7.

file

A vertical row of squares running between the two opponents. These rows are named by letters: a, b, c, d, e, f, g, and h.

forced move

A move that would lead to a lost position, if not made.

fork

All pieces and pawns are capable of forking. This special tactic by a single piece or pawn occurs when it attacks two or more of the opponent's pieces.

gambit

A proffered sacrifice, usually of a pawn, toward the opening of the game, intended to gain time or position. A gambit can be accepted (meaning your opponent takes the piece) or declined (meaning he doesn't take the piece).

grandmaster

The highest possible player rank in chess. Since 1950, this rank has been officially awarded by the FIDE (Fédération Internationale des Éches, or World Chess Federation), the governing body of world chess.

half-open file

A file that has a pawn of only one color on it is half open; the side without a pawn has a half-open file.

happy pieces and pawns

Any piece or pawn that is at full strength, making use of its potential.

J'adoube

French for "I adjust." A player, when it is his turn to move, may adjust (slide a chessman to the center of the square) pieces by first announcing "J'adoube" or "I adjust."

king

The most important piece in a chess game. When the king is trapped (this is called *checkmate*), the game is over, with the side that trapped his opponent's king victorious. This monarch moves one square at a time in any direction, and has the option once a game to castle.

king safety
Since he is the whole game, it makes sense to keep your king safe behind a wall of pawns until the danger of checkmate is much reduced.

kingside
The half of the board from the e-file to the h-file.

knight
Shaped like a horse's head, this chess piece leaps over all adjacent squares to a different-colored square. Each player gets two, and they begin the game between the bishops and the rooks.

long-range pieces
Queens, rooks, and bishops. These are pieces that can cover an entire open line in one move.

looking ahead
Visualizing a new position after one or more potential moves without actually disturbing the position.

major pieces
The rooks and queen; the pieces that have the potential for controlling the most squares.

mate
Short for checkmate.

mini-battery
A battery consisting of a queen or bishop as the base and a pawn as the front, lined up along the diagonal where the pawn can capture.

minor pieces
The bishops and knights; these pieces generally control fewer squares than the queen and rook.

no retreat
A situation in which a piece has nowhere safe to go.

notation
A system for recording the moves of a chess game.

open file
A file that has no pawns on it.

opening
The part of the game that is used to develop the pieces.

opposition
A technique used to force the opponent's king to move away by placing your king on a rank or file facing your opponent's king with one square in between.

passed pawn
A pawn that has no enemy pawns in front of it on the same file or on either adjacent file.

pawn promotion

When a piece reaches the final row on the opposite side of the board, it has the option of becoming a queen, rook, bishop, or knight.

pawns

The little guys that line up in front of the pieces at the start of a game. They have a distinctive type of move with many exceptions. Pawns have always been the foot soldiers of chess, and each player starts out with eight.

pieces

Kings, queens, rooks, bishops, and knights are the pieces in chess.

pin

A tactic that "sticks" or "pins down" one piece to another along a rank, file, or diagonal. If the piece is pinned to the king, it is illegal to move the pinned piece, for it would expose the king to check.

queen

Each player gets only one. She can move in any straight line, along ranks, files, or diagonals, any number of squares.

queenside

The half of the chessboard from the d-file to the a-file.

rank

A row that runs from left to right across the board. The numbered rows on marked chessboards.

removing the defender
A tactic that removes the defender of a given square, piece, or pawn, so that it is no longer defended.

rook
The rook moves along ranks or files, any number of squares, and is capable of castling with the king occasionally. It starts out in the corners when a game begins, and each player gets two.

sacrifice
Giving up material to gain a greater advantage. Often used for attacking the king.

skewer
The skewer is a backward pin. It is an attack on two pieces on the same rank, file, or diagonal, but, unlike the pin, it forces the closer piece to move, which leaves the other piece to be captured.

sleeping pieces
Pieces that have nothing to do, such as the long-range pieces at the start of a game.

stalemate
A tie game that results from the opponent with more material controlling all the squares around the weaker side's king but not directly attacking the king.

strategy
Strategy deals with overall plans or goals as opposed to tactical calculations.

tactics
The "fireworks" of chess. These are "tricks" or weapons used to win material or gain some other advantage. They include convergence, batteries, pins, forks, skewers, discovered attacks, removing defenders, no retreat, desperado, zwischenzug, and opposition.

tempo
An extra move. Usually you gain a tempo by forcing your opponent to move the same piece twice in a row.

threats
Any potential capture or promotion that will gain value, or any potential check, checkmate, stalemate, or other type of draw. All pieces and pawns are capable of making threats.

three-position repetition
A type of draw in which the same position, with the same player to move, is repeated for the third time during the course of a game.

touch move
In chess if you touch a piece without saying "I adjust" first, then you must move it.

tournament chess
An event where chess games are played against more than one opponent.

value of the pieces
The value of a piece depends on how many squares it attacks; therefore, the value will change depending upon where the piece is located on the board. Remember, however, your king is worth the game!

waking up the pieces
At the start of the game, all pieces are very sleepy (they have nothing to do). Waking them up means giving them lines and squares to go to so they can realize their potential strength.

White
The light pieces are referred to as White in chess, regardless of their actual color.

winning the Exchange
If you win a rook for a bishop or a knight, you have won the Exchange.

zugzwang
From the German, meaning that one is forced to move but has no good options.

zwischenzug
From the German, an in-between move.

Index